DEMONS IN THE SMOKE OF THE WORLD TRADE CENTER

The Invasion of Evil Spirits and the Blight of Islam

by

Dr. R. L. Hymers, Jr.

and

Dr. John S. Waldrip

Afterword by

U. S. Senator James M. Inhofe

DISCLAIMER

The people or sources mentioned in this book, as well as the endorsements, do not necessarily reflect the position of Dr. Hymers. Dr. Waldrip, or their respective churches.

+ +

Printed in the United States of America.

Published by:
Hearthstone Publishing, Ltd.
P. O. Box 815, Oklahoma City, OK 73101
405/789-3885   888/891-3300   FAX 405/789-6502

ISBN 1-57558-115-9

ABOUT THE AUTHORS

R. L. Hymers, Jr. is a graduate of the California State University at Los Angeles (B.A.), Golden Gate Baptist Theological Seminary, Southern Baptist (M.Div.), San Francisco Theological Seminary, United Presbyterian (D.Min.) and Louisiana Baptist Theological Seminary, Baptist Bible Fellowship (Th.D.). He and his wife Ileana are the parents of two sons. Dr. Hymers is the founding pastor of a Baptist church in Los Angeles. Known for his strong stand for Biblical inerrancy and inner-city evangelism, Dr. Hymers is an unashamed old-time fundamentalist. He has been in the ministry over forty-four years.

John S. Waldrip was appointed to the United States Air Force Academy in Colorado Springs, Colorado. He left the Air Force because of a physical injury. Waldrip holds a Bachelor of Science (B.S.) degree in mechanical engineering from Oregon State University. He is a graduate in theology from Pacific Coast Baptist Bible College, and holds a Doctor of Theology (Th.D.) from Louisiana Baptist Theological Seminary. He and his wife, Pam, are the parents of a daughter named Sarah. Dr. Waldrip is a strong advocate of old-time Biblical conversion. He has been the pastor of a Baptist church in Monrovia, California for seventeen years.

WEBSITES

Dr. Hymers' website is at www.rlhymersjr.com.
You can write to him at P. O. Box 15308,
Los Angeles, CA 90015.

Dr. Waldrip's website is at www.calvaryroadbaptist.org.
You can write to him at P. O. Box 15308,
Los Angeles, CA 90015.

DEDICATION

This book is dedicated to Iris Conner, an old-fashioned woman from Wheeler, Texas. Her legacy lies in the character of Dr. John S. Waldrip, who is very much his mother's son.

TABLE OF CONTENTS

Dr. Philip Schaff, renowned Christian historian, writes on Mohammed

(These quotations are from Philip Schaff, Ph.D., *A History of the Christian Church, volume IV*, Grand Rapids: William B. Eerdmans Publishing Co., 1976.)

"Among his last utterances were: 'The Lord destroy the Jews and Christians! Let his anger be kindled against those...Let there not remain any faith but that of Islam'" (p. 166).

"War against unbelievers is legalized by the Qu'ran [Koran]. The fighting men are to be slain, the women and children reduced to slavery. The violation of captive women of the enemy is the legitimate reward of the conqueror" (pp. 189-190).

"[Mohammed] believed in the use of the sword as the best missionary, and was utterly unscrupulous as to the means of success" (p. 169).

"'The sword,' says Mohammed, 'is the key of heaven and hell; a drop of blood shed in the cause of Allah, a night spent in arms, is of more avail than two months of fasting or prayer: whoever falls in battle, his sins are forgiven'" (p. 171).

"Mohammed was a slave of sensual passion...The motives of his excess in polygamy were his sensuality which grew with his years, and his desire for male offspring...He had at least fourteen legal wives, and a number of slave concubines besides. At his death he left nine widows. He claimed special revelations which gave him greater liberty in sexual indulgence than ordinary Moslems (who were restricted to four wives) and exempted him from the prohibition of marrying near relatives...Ayesha, the daughter of Abu Bakr, was his especial favorite. He married her when she was a girl of nine years, and he fifty-three years old" (pp. 169-170).

"To compare such a man with Jesus, is preposterous and even blasphemous. Jesus was the sinless Saviour of sinners; Mohammed was a sinner, and he knew and confessed it. He falls far below Moses, or Elijah, or any of the prophets and apostles in moral purity" (p. 171).

INTRODUCTION

Many books and articles have been published on the subject of Islam since September 11. But they do not deal with the subject like this book does – going beyond the headlines to expose the Satanic forces behind Muslim terrorism.

This book makes no apology for saying that the Islamic religion is demonic. We go into detail showing that Allah is actually an evil spirit, making it clear that those who practice Islam are under the control of demons. Our purpose is to show that these acts of terrorism are an attack against America by the Devil himself!

Dr. Jerry Vines' Statement Against Mohammed

The July 2002 Pastors' Conference of the Southern Baptist Convention featured a sermon by former SBC president Dr. Jerry Vines. Speaking to a vast crowd of Southern Baptist pastors, Dr. Vines made a strong statement against Islam, which is quoted in the following article:

> Comments by another [Pastors' Conference] speaker produced a swirl of controversy and prompted Islamic groups to demand an apology. Jerry Vines, pastor of First Baptist Church in Jacksonville, FL, cautioned the church not to succumb to religious materialism, humanism, and pragmatism. Americans today often hear that all religions are the same, Vines noted.
>
> "They would have you believe that Islam is as good as Christianity," he said. *"I am here to tell you Islam is not as good as Christianity. Christianity was founded by the virgin-born Jesus Christ. Islam was founded by Mohammed, a demon-possessed pedophile who had 12 wives, and his last one was a nine-year-old girl,"* Vines said to applause.
>
> *"Allah is not Jehovah, either,"* Vines said. *"Jehovah is not going to turn anyone into a terrorist that will try to bomb people and take the lives of thousands and thousands of people."* (Quoted in *The California Southern Baptist,* July 2002, p. 8).

1

Jerry Falwell's Defense of Vines

A media firestorm followed Dr. Vines' sermon. He was so viciously attacked in the newspapers and on television that Jerry Falwell felt he needed to give the following defense:

> In June, the annual meeting of the Southern Baptist Convention was met with some unexpected fireworks after my friend Dr. Jerry Vines, pastor of the First Baptist Church of Jacksonville, Fla., declared that Muhammad was a "demon-possessed pedophile" and that Islam teaches the destruction of all non-Muslims.
>
> If you want to raise the ire of the mainstream press and the swarm of politically-correct organizations in this nation, just criticize Islam (as Dr. Vines learned).
>
> Dr. Vines' statements were made in reference to the new book, "Unveiling Islam: An Insider's Look at Muslim Life and Beliefs" (Kregel Publications). It is written by scholars Ergun and Emir Caner, brothers raised as Muslims who are today dynamic and outspoken Christians. Ergun is assistant professor of theology and church history at Criswell College in Dallas, while Emir is assistant professor of church history and Anabaptist studies at Southeastern Baptist Theological Seminary in Wake Forest, N.C.
>
> Dr. Vines – who was, it should be noted, speaking in a private forum – also quoted from the Hadith, a trusted source for Islamic teachings among Muslim followers worldwide. The Caners say that *the Hadith verifies that Muhammad did indeed marry the nine-year-old daughter of a friend. The girl, named Aisha, became known as the "mother of believers."*
>
> *"It's simply a matter of quoting [Islamic] sources,"* said Emir Caner. *"If we are wrong in our understanding of the Islamic scriptures, we would be happy to be corrected."*
>
> *The specific Hadith citation concerning Muhammad's relationship with the young girl is in volume 7, book 6, number 64 and 65,* said Ergun Caner. (Both Emir and Ergun Caner were Sunni Muslims who became Christians in 1982).

2

"The comments in question cannot be considered bigotry when they come from Islamic writings," Ergun said during a press conference hosted by Baptist Press in St. Louis.

A passage from the Hadith, volume 1, book 1, chapter 1, shows that Muhammad himself believed he was under demonic influence, but it notes that Muhammad's wife is the one who deemed his experience as "divine," said Ergun.

Concerning terrorism and Islamic jihad, Emir noted that Muslims maintained diverse interpretations. Some, he said, see jihad as a "spiritual war," while others see it as meaning "physical."

"Some Muslims want to allegorize their own scriptures because they don't want to defend jihad," Emir said. "But if you take the Koran at its word, or Muhammad at his word, then you'll find physical jihad." In fact, he noted, the highest level of Muslim heaven – which has 70 perpetual virgins on couches – is reserved for Muslims who "shed their blood" (Hadith 135). Islam's inclination toward violence, he added, also is reflected in the Koran: "Slay the enemy where you find him" (Surah 9:92).

Dr. Vines was simply pointing out these distinctions. Since the media so often treats the Muslim religion with utter reverence – something we Baptists are unfamiliar with – he felt it was important that SBC members understand these distinctions. If those in the media were doing their jobs, Dr. Vines would have never felt it necessary to point out these disquieting elements of an enigmatic religion.

Ergun Caner observed an element of hypocrisy in the quest to portray Islam as a peaceful religion: *"A so-called Christian who bombs an abortion clinic or shoots an abortionist and says God told him to do it does that act against the Bible,"* he told Baptist Press. *"But the Muslim who commits acts of violence in jihad does so with the approval of Muhammad... When September 11 happened, we were all shocked. But where was the international outrage when jihad killed three million people (Christian people, I might add) in Sudan?"* (Dr. Jerry Falwell, *National Liberty Journal*, July 2002, pp. 2-3).

The points which Dr. Vines and Dr. Falwell brought out are explained in detail in the book you are about to read.

John Ashcroft and John of Damascus Agree – Allah and God are Not the Same

John of Damascus (c.675-c.749 A.D.) wrote that the main difference between Christianity and Islam lies in the view of Jesus Christ held by the two religions. Dr. Samuel Hugh Moffett is emeritus professor of missions at Princeton Theological Seminary. Dr. Moffett says,

> To John [of Damascus], the crucial difference is this: the God of the Muslims is not the Christian God: Allah had no son. John's God is the Father of Jesus Christ (Samuel Hugh Moffett, Ph.D., "Divided by Christ," *Christian History* magazine, Issue 74, May 2002, p. 40).

Attorney General John Ashcroft made a similar statement according to newspaper columnist Cal Thomas,

> Islam is a religion in which God requires you to send *your* son to die for him. Christianity is a faith in which God sends *His* Son to die for you (*Christianity Today,* April 1, 2002).

The book you are about to read ties together all of these themes and presents a comprehensive view of Islam as a demonic religion which has been unleashed against America. In this time of spiritual darkness, we believe that the message of our book will help to shed light on the work of Satan and his demons through the Muslim religion.

R. L. Hymers, Jr. and
John S. Waldrip
July 4, 2002

Part I

THE INVASION OF EVIL SPIRITS

by

Dr. R. L. Hymers, Jr.

CHAPTER 1
SATAN ATTACKS AMERICA

I believe that Satan and demons are behind the terrorist attacks on America. One of the tabloids published a large photograph of the blasted World Trade Center, showing what appeared to be the face of Satan in the bellowing black and grey plumes of smoke. The "face" that hung in the smoke had evil looking eyes, a pointed beard, and the horns of a Satanic figure (*Globe*, October 6, 2001, pp. 1-2). The magazine said it appeared to be "the hideous face of the devil himself."

I would not want to make a definite statement about this photograph, and I do not think there is anything particularly supernatural about it. Yet it was certainly a reminder that there really is a Devil – and demons actually exist. These evil beings are spoken of throughout the Bible. In my opinion, the Devil and his demons are behind the terrorist attacks on our nation. You could literally "feel" the demonic presence as you watched those planes fly into the World Trade Center on your TV screen.

The Bible has a great deal to say about Satanic forces. And I am convinced that we need to know what it says about these malignant spirits if we want to understand what is behind these terrorist attacks.

A Spiritual Federation

The Scriptures teach that demons form a federation of evil, under the leadership of Satan. The Bible speaks of "the devil and his angels" (Matthew 25:41). The Scriptures tell us that Satan has a kingdom (ref. Matthew 12:26-27), and the demons are his subjects. They are his emissaries and agents, in his realm of spiritual darkness. The kingdom of Satan is very strong and very large. We must never underestimate the power and greatness of his empire.

When Christ was tempted in the wilderness, we are told:

> "The devil taketh him up into an exceeding high mountain, and sheweth him all the kingdoms of the world, and the glory of them; And saith unto him, All these things will I give thee, if thou wilt fall down and worship me" (Matthew 4:8-9).

6

The parallel passage in Luke gives us further information:

> "And the devil, taking him up into an exceeding high mountain, shewed unto him all the kingdoms of the world in a moment of time. And the devil said unto him, All this power will I give thee, and the glory of them, *for that is delivered unto me; and to whomsoever I will I give it*" (Luke 4:5-6).

Taken together, these two accounts show us the great power given to the Devil. The passages show also that the Devil controls the nations of the world. That's why the Scriptures call the Devil, "the prince of the power of the air" in Ephesians 2:2. He is in control of the airways. He is also called, "the god of this world" (II Corinthians 4:4). These verses reveal that Satan dominates this world system, and is in control of the airways, where earth's atmosphere exists. It should not surprise us, then, that Satan led wicked men in airplanes to destroy the World Trade Center. He is the master of the airways. He is the god of this world – and therefore the god who destroyed the World Trade Center and the Pentagon.

The Devil told Christ that "the world is delivered unto me; and to whomsoever I will give it" (Luke 4:6). This means that God is sovereign. God is supreme. But God has "delivered" this sinful world to Satan. God has allowed the Devil to control the airways and the world-system. Therefore, it was Satan who was behind the destruction of these buildings. Satan and his demons were in back of these acts of terrorism.

Demon Possession

The Bible teaches that people can be demon possessed.

> "When the even was come, they brought unto him many that were possessed with devils (i.e. demons): and he cast out the spirits with his word..." (Matthew 8:16).

> "And when he was come to the other side into the country of the Gergesenes, there met him two possessed with devils (i.e. demons), coming out of the tombs, exceeding fierce, so that no man might pass by that way" (Matthew 8:28).

7

> "As we went to prayer, a certain damsel [i.e. young girl] possessed with a spirit of divination met us..." (Acts 16:16).

Demon possession is the only way to account for the behavior of many people today. The wickedness that they practice can only be explained on the basis of demon possession. Take for example the people who flew those airplanes into the World Trade Center and the Pentagon. They were highly intelligent men with good educations. Yet they mindlessly committed suicide to attack those buildings. How can such actions be explained apart from demon possession?

The Bible teaches that Satan and his demons will exert great influence over many people in the last days, before the end of the world as we know it. It says, "In the latter times some shall depart from the faith, giving heed to seducing spirits, and doctrines of devils..." (I Timothy 4:1). The Bible teaches that demon activity will be particularly strong among world rulers:

> "For they are the spirits of devils [demons], working miracles, which go forth unto the kings of the earth and of the whole world..." (Revelation 16:14).

I believe that Hitler and Stalin and Mao Tse Tung were demon possessed. I believe that Osama bin Laden, Saddan Hussein, and Moammar Gadhafi are demon possessed. I believe that the Taliban leaders of Afghanistan were controlled by demons, and so are the terrorists attacking America! Led by Satan, demonic powers are attacking us through these people, whom they dominate and use as puppets to carry out their evil plans.

Demonic Maladies

Demons often inflict physical maladies. Notice how the demons harmed people when Christ was on earth:

> "And his fame went throughout all Syria: and they brought unto him all sick people that were taken with divers diseases and torments, and those which were possessed with devils [demons], and those which were lunatick, and those that had the palsy, and he healed them" (Matthew 4:24).

8

A man came to Jesus and said:

> "Lord, have mercy on my son: for he is lunatick, and
> sore vexed: for ofttimes he falleth into the fire, and oft
> into the water...And Jesus rebuked the devil [demon];
> and he departed out of him..." (Matthew 17:15-18).

Demons not only inflict disease, they can also produce great strength and fierceness:

> "And when he was come to the other side...there met
> him two possessed with devils, coming out of the
> tombs, exceeding fierce, so that no man might pass by
> that way" (Matthew 8:28).

The enormous fierceness and fury of Muslim terrorists reminds me of these demon possessed men, who lived in the tombs at the time of Christ.

But we must be careful to notice that these terrorists are not the only people who are under the influence of demons. The Bible tells us that every unconverted person is controlled to some degree by the demonic:

> "Wherein in time past ye walked according to the course
> of this world, according to the prince of the power of
> the air, the spirit that now worketh in the children of
> disobedience" (Ephesians 2:2).

The "prince of the power of the air" in this verse is Satan. And the verse tells us that he "worketh in the children of disobedience."

Jesus once told a group of people He encountered:

> "Ye are of your father the devil, and the lusts of your
> father ye will do..." (John 8:44).

The Devil tempts, twists, and leads people into sin. Those who are not converted are in "the snare of the devil, who are taken captive by him at his will" (II Timothy 2:26). The Devil can get such a hold on you that you become his slave. No one but Jesus Christ can set you free from the clutches of Satan.

Demons are the Enemy

We should always remember that Satan and his demons are the real enemy. The Bible says:

> "For we wrestle not against flesh and blood, but against...spiritual wickedness in high places" (Ephesians 6:12).

That's what Daniel learned also. The real enemy was no human being. It was Satan and the demons:

> "But the prince of the kingdom of Persia withstood me one and twenty days" (Daniel 10:13).

It was a demon called "the prince of the kingdom of Persia" who withstood Daniel and hindered his prayers.

It's important for true Christians to know who we are fighting. It isn't people. It's demonic forces. The *people* who come against us are only his tools and his instruments. Remembering that will keep you from becoming bitter at Muslims, and other people who attack you and are unkind to you. We can learn to love our enemies when we realize that they are merely slaves of the Devil!

The English word "demon" is a translation of the Greek word "daimōn." It is mistranslated as "devils" in the King James Bible. It should always be translated as "demons." The Greek word in the New Testament comes from the root "da," which means "to know." So, the word "demon" means "a knowing one." The classical philosopher Plato said the word means "knowing" or "intelligent" (George P. Pardington, Ph.D., *Outline Studies in Christian Doctrine*, Christian Publications, 1926, p. 122).

Demons are called "the knowing ones" because they *know a great deal.* After all, they have been roaming the earth for thousands of years. If you had been travelling around the world for as long as they have, you would know a great deal also! Yes, the demons are very intelligent, and well informed, and very cunning. You will never be able to outsmart them, because they are too sly and crafty. They will outsmart you every time. That's why you need Jesus Christ, and the Bible, and the local church. You will never be able to outsmart the demons by yourself. They will get you and drag you down to Hell!

Now the Bible gives many answers concerning demons. Here are three important questions about these evil spirits that are dealt with by the Scriptures.

Where did Demons Come From?

The Bible teaches that Satan was once a great archangel in Heaven named Lucifer. But he rebelled against God. He said, "I will ascend above the heights of the clouds; I will be like the most High" (Isaiah 14:14). He was cast out of Heaven into the atmosphere of the earth. After he was cast out of Heaven, Lucifer became known as Satan, or the Devil.

Now when Satan first rebelled against God, before he was cast out of Heaven, a great many of the angels followed him. There was a "church split" in Heaven. Lucifer and his angels rebelled against God and His angels. And when God threw Satan out of Heaven, He cast the rebellious angels out with him. *And that's exactly what needs to happen in many of our churches. They need a "back door revival"! Those that are causing division need to leave. Then the church will be like Heaven!*

The Bible says:

> "God spared not the angels that sinned, but cast them down to hell, and delivered them into chains of darkness, to be reserved unto judgment" (II Peter 2:4).

Again, the Scriptures say:

> "The angels which kept not their first estate, but left their own habitation, he hath reserved in everlasting chains under darkness unto the judgment of the great day" (Jude 6).

So, many of the "fallen angels" were consigned directly to Hell.

Yet other angels who were cast out of Heaven remained in the atmosphere, in the air around the earth. Here are my convictions on this subject.

Some of the demons possessed people in the days of Noah. I believe that the "sons of God" in Job 1:6; 2:1; 38:7 were fallen angels. These "sons of God" "came in unto the daughters of men" in Noah's day (Genesis 6:4). These demons were then cast into Hell.

That's why the demons who were confronted by Jesus "besought him that he would not command them to go out into the deep" (Luke 8:31) because they too had possessed a human being.

So, the angels which rebelled were cast out onto the earth. Those that sinned even farther by possessing human beings were cast "into the deep" (Luke 8:31).

But many of these demons remain on the earth today. They are the ones who did not possess human beings in the days before the Flood. And the Bible teaches that the leader of these demons is Satan (cf. Matthew 12:26-27; Matthew 25:41; Revelation 12:9). That's where the demons come from.

Demonic Phenomena

Dr. Henry C. Thiessen was the late Chairman of the Faculty of the Graduate School at Wheaton College. Dr. Thiessen gave a list of things that demons do:

1. They inflict disease [not all disease, but certain diseases], Job 1:5-10; Matthew 9:33; 12:22; Luke 9:37-42; 13:11,16.

2. They cause mental disorders [not all, but many], Mark 5:4,5; Luke 8:35.

3. They lead many into moral impurity, Matthew 10:1; 12:43; Mark 1:23-27; 3:11; 5:2-13; Luke 4:33,36; 6:18; 8:29; Acts 5:16; 8:7; Revelation 16:13.

4. They disseminate [spread] false doctrine, I Kings 22:21-23; II Thessalonians 2:2; I Timothy 4:1.

5. They oppose God's children, Ephesians 6:12.

6. They sometimes possess human beings and even animals, Matthew 4:24; Mark 5:8-14; Luke 8:2; Acts 8:7; 16:16.

7. They are sometimes used by God in the carrying out of His purposes and designs, Judges 9:23; I Samuel 16:14; Psalm 78:49. It appears that He will especially so use them during the Tribulation period, Revelation 9:1-12; 16:13-16. They will

apparently be invested with miraculous powers for the time being, II Thessalonians 2:9; Revelation 16:14.

8. They are behind fortune telling and astrology, Isaiah 47:13; Acts 16:16. When the destiny of a person is shown ahead of time, it is the work of demons.

9. They are behind spiritualism [or spiritism] – the belief that the living can communicate with the dead, which is also called necromancy. A necromancer is often referred to in the Bible as someone who has "a familiar spirit," Leviticus 19:31; Deuteronomy 18:11; I Samuel 28:3,7,8,9; II Kings 21:6; 23:24; etc. (Henry C. Thiessen, Ph.D., *Lectures in Systematic Theology*, Eerdmans, 1963, pp. 208-209).

The Bible warns Christians not to be ignorant of Satan's devices (ref. II Corinthians 2:11).

Dr. John Nevius, in his classical book *Demon Possession and Allied Themes* (Revell, 1894, pp. 321-322), gives the following list of demonic phenomena:

1. The use of a medium for the purpose of holding communication with spirits.

2. Necromancy, or professed communication with the dead by the intervention of a medium.

3. The invoking or summoning of spirits by means of hymns or prayer.

4. Reeceiving communications from spirits by writing, through methods more or less direct and immediate.

5. Gradual "development" or training by which the medium or subject, and the spirits, are brought [in contact], so that the medium becomes ready and responsive in performing his new functions.

6. Obtaining prescriptions and healing diseases by spirits, through the intervention of a medium.

7. Carrying on communications with spirits through a medium by the use of spoken language, or by raps, or other arrangements or devices.

8. The mysterious appearance and disappearance of...lights and flames.

9. Levitation, suspension in the air, and transference from one place to the other of crockery, household utensils, and other objects, including also men...

10. Haunted houses, mysterious opening and shutting of doors, and other similar phenomena.

11. The moving of furniture and other objects without physical contact.

12. Rappings, clattering of dishes, and unusual noises and disturbances, without any physical cause which can be found.

13. Impressions by unseen hands, sometimes gentle, sometimes violent, producing physical pain and injuries.

14. The nervous and muscular symptoms peculiar to a demoniac, and often to the medium during possession, or its initial stage.
    (Nevius, ibid., pp. 321-322).

Dr. Nevius continued by saying, "The Bible teaches us that to have intercourse with a 'familiar' spirit is a voluntary act of disloyalty to, and rebellion against God. It is forsaking God, and holding intercourse with, and becoming the agent of his avowed enemy, the devil" (Nevius, ibid., p. 323).

Why Learn about Demonology?

Theologian August H. Strong was wrong about some things, but he was correct in giving us four main "uses of the doctrine of evil angels" (Augustus H. Strong, D.D., *Systematic Theology*, Judson

Press, 1985, p. 463). He says that there are four main reasons we should know about demons:

1. "[Demonology] illustrates the real nature of sin, and the depth of the ruin to which it may bring the soul, to [think about] the present moral condition and eternal wretchedness to which these spirits...have brought themselves by their rebellion against God."

   The demons have indeed ruined themselves and cursed themselves by rebelling against God. You should think deeply about that. If *you* go on missing church and rejecting Jesus Christ, *you too* will be eternally cut off from God and damned to Hell.

2. "[Demonology] inspires a [healthy, safe] fear and hatred of the...subtle approaches of evil from within and without, to remember that these may be the...advances of a personal and malignant being, who seeks to overcome [us], and involve us in his own apostasy and destruction."

   By thinking about what Satan and demons do, you will be reminded that they are out to destroy you. This knowledge will help you overcome temptation and sin. If you realize that demonic activity is present, you will want to read the Bible, be in church, and pray.

3. "[Demonology] shuts us up to Christ, as the only being who is able to deliver us or others from the enemy of all good."

   Many people do not see why they need Christ because they do not realize that He is the only one who can save them from being damned to Hell through the temptations and sin that Satan and the demons bring to them. Biblical thinking concerning demons turns a person fully to the only Saviour, Jesus Christ.

4. "[Demonology] teaches us that our salvation is wholly of grace, since for such multitudes of rebellious spirits no atonement and no renewal were provided...with no mercy to interpose or save."

Christ did not die on the Cross as a payment for the sins of demons. But He did die on the Cross to pay for *your* sins. This means that you have an opportunity to be saved. You have an opportunity that no demon has. They are bound to go to Hell. But *you* could be saved by turning fully to Jesus Christ, the Son of God. (Strong, ibid.).

Allah Is a Demon

It doesn't take much knowledge of the Bible to see that the "Allah" of Islam is actually Satan. As we will show in the pages that follow, those who worship Allah often become demon-possessed. That is the reason for the fanaticism, the suicide bombings, and other destructive acts. America is actually waging war with demons, and with Satan himself!   We have little hope of winning this battle without the help of God.

Demonic powers oppose God and the work of Christ on earth. This is clearly shown to us in the book of Daniel:

> "But the prince of the kingdom of Persia withstood me one and twenty days" (Daniel 10:13).

There was a three-week delay in God answering Daniel's prayer. The reason for this delay was the opposition of a demon called "the price of Persia."   This passage of Scripture shows us that Satan has demonic powers which can motivate whole nations to stand against God (ref. Ephesians 6:12). We need to pray hard and long for God to deliver our nation from these evil spiritual forces.

CHAPTER 2
HOW DEMONS HAVE GOTTEN
CONTROL OF OUR NATION

In October, 2001 the American Civil Liberties Union (ACLU) brought a lawsuit against a public school in northern California for displaying the words "God Bless America" on a sign board in front of the school. The ACLU said the words "God Bless America" were illegal and "inspire hatred and division." At any other moment in history, their statement would have seemed insane. Yet many secularists in America agree with them today.

Let's untwist the thinking of the ACLU and their supporters by asking two questions and then answering them. First, who is offended by the words "God Bless America"? Certainly not the Christians, either Catholic or Protestant, in any denomination. Certainly not any practicing Jew. After all, the words "God Bless America" come to us directly from the song of that title, written in 1939 by Irving Berlin, a practicing Jew. No mainstream Muslim in America would be offended by these words either, for they profess to believe in one god, whom they call Allah. Nor would a Buddhist or Hindu be offended by these words, since "God" is not defined in the slogan, and could be interpreted by them to refer to their deities. Even reasonable agnostics should not be offended by the slogan, since an agnostic merely says that he is not *sure* whether there is a God or not. He is not against believing in God, but only unsure of His existence. Therefore a reasonable agnostic would not be alarmed at a harmless slogan that merely calls on an unspecified deity to bless his nation in a time of terrorism.

Second, who then is offended? Only a very small group of militant atheists! They compose less than one percent of the American people! Why should over 99% of our people have to give in to this tiny group? After all, our nation is a democracy, which means (though they don't want us to remember it) that the majority of people are supposed to decide things – not a tiny group of vicious God-haters, backed up by highly paid attorneys! Why don't they let the people vote for things like this? I think it is because they know that the American people would vote overwhelmingly to put prayer back in the schools if it were put on a ballot and decided democratically. In the name of tolerance and love, the ACLU tells us that the slogan "God Bless America" causes "hatred and division." I say, poppycock, tomfoolery, "professing themselves to be wise, they became fools" (Romans 1:22).

In case you hadn't noticed, the ACLU and their secularist backers are Hell-bent on removing *any* mention of God, and especially His Son, Jesus, from public life in our nation. And when they have succeeded, then I believe they will go *into* our churches and tell us what we can or can't say there as well. I have news for them. This is one Baptist preacher who will never give in to a secular purging of God from his church. *They will tell me what to say in the pulpit over my dead body - and in no other way!*

They have removed all mention of Christmas and Easter from our public schools – but they allow these same schools to celebrate Halloween, the Devil's birthday. They reject God, and they reject Christ, but they urge every public school child to celebrate the demonic holiday of Halloween. How did such a twisting of religious expression come about in American life? Let us consider that question carefully.

America Once Knew God

If the public schools taught a little more U.S. History instead of so much sex education you would already know what I'm going to tell you. I don't blame you. It isn't your fault. It's the fault of the secularists, who have removed nearly all mention of our Judeo-Christian heritage from the books you read in public schoolrooms.

But I'm here to tell you that America was founded by people who believed the Bible. References to the Bible are all through the Declaration of Independence and the Constitution of the United States. Our coins have "In God We Trust" imprinted on them. These words are also printed on our paper money. Every President takes his oath of office with his right hand placed on a Bible, and promises to defend the Constitution and the nation with the words, "So help me God." Words of Scripture are written on the walls of the Capitol in Washington, D.C., and on many other public buildings there. A minister opens every session of Congress with prayer. Another chaplain opens every session of the United States Senate with prayer. These practices go back over two hundred years, to the very beginning of our nation.

Presidents, Congressmen, and Senators begin their work days with authorized public prayer. But the ACLU says that our children cannot do the same thing, that it "inspires hatred and division" if they do. Yet I clearly remember praying in the third grade in public school in Arizona, when I was a child. I also remember participating in a Christmas play, as one of the wise men, in a Los Angeles public school when I was a child - and no one thought anything about it! We had *far* less hatred and violence back then, in the 1940s, than we do since God has been banned from our school rooms!

The secularists now tell us that all of this was "unconstitutional." I have always found it absurd that *no one* thought of that before the 1960s, including Thomas Jefferson, who took his oath of office as President with his hand on a Bible, and said, "So help me God" – and never once complained about being required to do so! And Thomas Jefferson never said anywhere, even in private conversation, that prayer in a school room was unconstitutional. *Thomas Jefferson was in complete agreement that prayer and Bible study should take place in every classroom in America. If he had said even one word against it the secularists would be trumpeting it at every opportunity!*

It took Madalyn Murray O'Hair to tell us what Jefferson never said, that kids can't pray in a school room. No one before O'Hair, backed by the ACLU, ever thought it was wrong or said so. O'Hair's own son, whom she put up in court as a little boy to say he didn't want to pray, has now retracted his statement. He says repeatedly now that his mother was wrong, that she was a Communist sympathizer, and did not correctly interpret the Constitution. I say that her son is right – and the ACLU and his mother were *dead* wrong!

Yes, she is now dead. One of her secularist "friends" chopped her to pieces and buried her body parts in a remote area of Texas. That's what she got from this secularist who backed her up in removing God from our schools! We have been disintegrating as a nation ever since prayer was banned from the public school rooms. I know that is true because I was there when it happened. As my mother used to say, "I was there, Charlie!"

America Became Vain in its Imaginations

In 1845 hordes of Irish immigrants began pouring into the United States as a result of the potato famine in Ireland. This wave of immigration brought millions of Roman Catholics into the great cities of America for the first time. Previously our nation had been overwhelmingly Protestant. Many of the Irish Catholics could have been won over by Protestants and Baptists at this time, but the Protestants and Baptists began to retreat from the cities. Instead of winning the lost, they began to withdraw to the countryside.

That has been going on for the past 150 years. In the twentieth century Fundamental Christianity became largely a rural and backwoods religion as a result. For instance, Prattville, Alabama has a population of 28,000 people and has three (3) churches listed in the Baptist Bible Fellowship directory, while Manhattan, New York has zero (0) churches listed. So, in Prattville, Alabama, there is one BBF church for about every 9,000 people, but Manhattan, New York has *not one* BBF church for two million people! Hutchinson, Kansas has a population of 39,000 and has seven churches listed in the directory. Los Angeles, with a population of four million, has two churches listed. Our church, the Fundamentalist Baptist Tabernacle, is the only BBF church located in the central city of Los Angeles. So, Hutchinson, Kansas has one BBF church for about every 5½ thousand people, while Los Angeles has *only two* churches for *four million* people! When preachers gather to plan a new church, they target a far-away suburb, way out in Canyon Country, or deep in Orange County. It doesn't seem to enter their minds to start a church among the four million unreached people of Los Angeles. One preacher said to me, "There aren't any people in Los Angeles now." What he meant was, "There aren't any *white* people." But even that statement is untrue.

I am not saying this to attack anyone, but as an exhortation. I am encouraging our preachers to send someone to help reach this city! Every great metropolis in America needs to have "home missionaries." Send some missionaries to our own cities before we have anarchy in the streets! It's a terrible shame that wasn't done long ago! We just haven't done our job!

And that is the story of conservative Protestants and Baptists in America. Our churches retreated from Boston, New York, San Francisco, Los Angeles, and other large cities, out into the countryside. We left the cities to be taken over by the Roman Catholics and the cults.

In 1890 evangelist D. L. Moody said, "We must reach the cities if we want to have a Christian nation," but few people listened to him.

We kept starting churches out in Prattville, Alabama; Berryville, Arkansas; Poppyseed, Kansas; and Pumpville, Texas – while we let the great cities go to Hell, without lifting a finger to save them!

We also retreated from the intellectual life of our nation. We withdrew from running the newspapers and the universities. We allowed atheists, Communists and "free thinkers" to take over the media and entertainment industries. We then sat mindlessly for hours every night in front of our TVs and let them pump their sewage through our brains by the hour.

With the Bible-believing Christians hiding out in Pumpville, Texas, America was overrun with pagan religion and atheism - and nothing practical was done to reverse the situation.

Oh, evangelicals occasionally attended a Billy Graham crusade, or another so-called "evangelistic meeting," where they marched the church kids forward so they could pronounce them "saved" – a short time before they left the church for good. Evangelicals then called them "backslidden" when they didn't attend church for thirty years. This was the "decisionist" response to a nation rapidly turning away from God.

America Became a Nation of Fools

When people reject the truth of the Bible the darkness of spiritual falsehood comes in like a flood. Men become fools by believing their own philosophies about God, the universe, and life itself.

The fourth century historian Eusebius tells us that the oldest civilizations did not worship idols. Persia, Rome, Greece, Egypt, and China had no idols when they began. But Romans 1:21-32 shows the downward spiral these civilizations took - going from light to darkness. And that is the same path America is taking today.

> "Because that, when they knew God, they glorified him not as God, neither were thankful; but became vain in their imaginations, and their foolish heart was darkened. *Professing themselves to be wise, they became fools"* (Romans 1:21-22).

America has descended from a nation of Pilgrims and Puritans into a nation of pagans who seldom attend church. We have gone from a

21

nation that celebrated Thanksgiving with prayer, to a nation where even the adults dress up like ghouls and demons on Halloween. We have gone from Thanksgiving to God to the exaltation of Satan in less than two hundred years! We have turned from being a nation where every school child was taught the Bible, and have become a nation where the birth of Christ and Easter cannot even be mentioned – but where every school child is encouraged to glorify Satan at Halloween – in the school room! *We have become a nation of fools* (ref. Romans 1:22).

Why have we turned away from God and embraced the Satanic idols of Halloween? Why do our people glory in Halloween rather than Jesus Christ? The Bible gives a simple answer:

> "Men loved darkness rather than light, because their deeds were evil. For every one that doeth evil hateth the light..." (John 3:19-20).

People who are evil hate the light of Christmas and Easter. They hate the light of Jesus Christ. They even hate the light of the slogan "God Bless America."

One teenager told me recently, "They didn't care when I ran out, took drugs, and partied all night. But now they are angry because I want to come to church." Another teenager was thrown out of his home for coming to our church. He told his mother, "I need God." But his mother said, "I'm your God!" And she threw him out of his own home! Parents like that are absolutely evil!

> "Professing themselves to be wise, they became fools" (Romans 1:22).

If you become a real Christian in these dark days someone is going to be upset with you.

Several years ago, when I was pastoring in northern California, a girl came to our church and got saved. She had been a hippie. She had taken drugs and done many other sinful things. But someone brought her to our church and she got saved. When she cleaned up her life and became a Christian her mother became furious and threatened to kick her out of the home. I heard about that and went to the woman's house to reason with her. It was an expensive home in a rich neighborhood in Marin County, near San Francisco. The mother invited me in and gave me a chair. She sat down on the sofa, and

22

looked at me with an angry face. Then she said this about her daughter, "When she became a hippie, I could handle it. When she took drugs and ran around with boys, I could handle it. But now she has become a Christian - and I cannot and will not stand for it!" She spewed out the word "Christian" like it was the most horrible, vile thing her daughter could have become! "Now she has become a *Christian* – I cannot and will not stand for it!" I couldn't calm her down. As I left her house I could smell hard liquor on her breath. A few days later she did throw the teenager out for becoming a Christian. The girl moved in with some people from the church and grew into a strong Christian woman. The last I heard of her, she had gone out as a missionary for Christ.

That girl made the right choice, but it was a hard one for a new Christian to make. It cost her the affection of her mother, and her home, to become a real follower of Christ. Jesus said:

> "He that loveth father or mother more than me is not worthy of me: and he that loveth son or daughter more than me, is not worthy of me. And he that taketh not his cross, and followeth after me, is not worthy of me" (Matthew 10:37-38).

If you become a true Christian, someone in your family may be very upset. Count the cost. Jesus said that if you become a real Christian, "A man's foes [enemies] shall be they of his own household" (Matthew 10:36).

Is it worth it? *You bet it is!* Jesus suffered, bled, and died on the Cross to pay for your sins. If you come to know Christ, your sins will be cancelled out – washed away by His Blood. And Christ arose physically from the dead. He is alive, seated on the right hand of God in Heaven – praying for you. If you put your full trust in Jesus, the Son of God, you will have eternal life. *Yes, it is worth whatever it costs you to become a real Christian!*

The Halloween Connection

As America plunges into spiritual darkness a growing number of people are participating in Halloween activities we never dreamed of when I was a child. There is an ever-increasing fascination with "ghosts" and magic.

Thousands of people attended a blockbuster movie about a haunted house a few months ago. This ghost story was titled "The Others." I do *not* recommend this movie. I don't think you should even see the video. But I can tell you this much about it, from MovieRevue@Hollywood.com:

> Nicole Kidman plays the role of Grace in this supernatural suspense thriller about a young woman and her two children living in a secluded house on the Channel Islands [off of the Coast of England]. Grace's daughter claims to see apparitions, which lead her to believe there are intruders at large in the house...[ghosts in the attic - and roaming through the empty rooms of the floors above them].
>
> It's 1945, and Grace's husband, Charles (Christopher Eccleston), went off to fight in World War II and never came back. She is therefore left alone to raise her two children, Anne (Alakina Mann) and Nicholas (James Bentley), in a cavernous Victorian mansion engulfed in gloom and fog on the Isle of Jersey. Following the German Occupation, the family learned to live without electricity, which worked to their advantage since the youngsters suffer a rare allergy to light and cannot be exposed to any light brighter than a candle. The three new servants, Mrs. Mills (Fionnula Flanagan), Mr. Tuttle (Eric Sykes) and Lydia (Elaine Cassidy) are carefully briefed by Grace about the importance of closing and locking every door in the house. The light, she explains, must be locked out like water from room to room. The religiously repressed Grace is also prone to migraine attacks and insists the house must be kept in absolute silence at all times. When Anne begins to complain that she see ghosts in the house, Grace tells the servants, "My children sometimes have strange ideas, but you mustn't listen to them. Children will be children." Eventually, however, she begins to believe that perhaps there are others living amongst them in the house.

I don't think *anyone* should see this film. Like "The Exorcist," this sort of movie is spiritual pornography. When something frightens you as much as these movies it could open you up to demonic influence – and perhaps even demon possession. Stay away from anything that makes your flesh crawl with terror. It isn't good for you to see movies like "The Others."

But there is a fascination with death, and with "spirits" that drew hundreds of thousands of people to theaters – to see this bone-chilling ghost story.

The Bible tells us that a man named Eliphaz was confronted by a spirit. It was very late at night. He was asleep. Suddenly fear gripped him. He began to tremble because he sensed that a supernatural force had entered his room in the darkness. He said:

> "Fear came upon me, and trembling, which made all my bones to shake. Then a spirit passed before my face; the hair of my flesh stood up: It stood still, but I could not discern the form thereof: an image was before mine eyes, there was silence, and I heard a voice..." (Job 4:14-16).

The German Bible scholars Keil and Delitzsch give this comment:

> The subject...is the undiscerned ghostlike something. Eliphaz was stretched upon his bed when a breath of wind passed over his face...His hair bristled up, even every hair of his body, [with] the ghostlike appearance as subject. He could not discern its outline, only the most ethereal form was before his eyes, and he heard, as it were proceeding from it, a voice, which spoke to him in a gentle, whispering tone... (C. F. Keil and F. Delitzsch, *Commentary on the Old Testament*, Volume IV, Eerdmans, 1973, p. 93).

Bible commentators Jamieson, Fausset and Brown add these observations:

> At first the apparition [ghost, specter, or phantom, *Webster*] glides before Eliphaz, then stands still, but with that shadowy indistinctness of a form which creates such an impression of awe; a gentle murmur! (Jamieson, Fausset and Brown, *A Commentary on the Old and New Testaments*, vol. 2, Eerdmans, reprint, 1976, p. 9).

25

John MacArthur calls this specter, "A mysterious messenger" (*MacArthur Study Bible,* comment on Job 4:12-16).
Do I believe that this actually happened? Yes, I do. Do I believe that Eliphaz experienced something supernatural and weird? Yes, I do. *Do I believe that it was a ghost? No, I do not!*
The Bible teaches that there are no such things as ghosts. Human spirits do *not* roam the earth after death according to the Bible. Then what *was* the "spirit" that "passed before" the face of Eliphaz and made his hair stand on end? *I am convinced that it was a demon.*
The Bible teaches that demons are very real. Dr. Merrill F. Unger, of Dallas Theological Seminary, said:

> There is not a hint that Jesus or any of the New Testament writers had the slightest doubt as to the real existence of either Satan or demons. They believed in their reality quite as much as in the existence of God, or the good angels (Merrill F. Unger, *Biblical Demonology*, Scripture Press, 1952, p. 36).

To the materialist, who denies the reality of demons and angels, Shakespeare said:

> "There are more things in heaven and earth, Horatio,
> Than are dreamt of in your philosophy."

Yes, the Bible teaches that demons are very real. And one of the things demons do is deceive people. Jesus told us that the Devil is a liar in John 8:44. The Devil and his demons lie to people, so they can tempt them to sin and lead them to destruction. And demons *pretend* to be ghosts to deceive people into thinking that they are spirits of the departed dead.
Dr. Kurt Koch, a German Bible teacher, gives this account in one of his books on the occult:

> When I was preaching in Edmonton, [Alberta] Canada, a twenty-one-year-old girl came to me for counselling. She said that at night the doors in her house would open. The radio turned on by itself. She could hear footsteps, scratching and knocking noises, see gleams of light and faces, hear voices and [see] transparent people walking back and forth, even though all the doors were locked. She was not suffering from a mental disorder. I told her that there were spiritists

26

either in the house or among her ancestors. She admitted this. Her grandmother had been a charmer and a spiritist and had died in terrible circumstances (Kurt Koch, Th.D., *Occult ABC*, Literature Mission, Germany, 1983, pp. 230-231).

As Dr. Koch points out, demons *pretend* to be the "ghosts" of dead people. Now, why would demons do such a thing? Why would they pretend to be ghosts?

Demons Pretend to be Ghosts
To Make People Think There Is No Hell

The Devil is a liar and the father of it (ref. John 8:44). He knows perfectly well that Hell is real. In fact, Satan knows that Hell was originally prepared for him and for his demons (ref. Matthew 25:41).

Yes, the Devil and his demons know there is a Hell. They are not in Hell now, but they know that God will send them there in the future. But these *demons do not want you to believe in Hell.* That's one of the main reasons that demons pretend to be ghosts. You see, if human spirits roam the world, and haunt houses, then the Bible isn't true, and there is no Hell.

America has become so demonically controlled that we no longer think about Hell, but we see pictures of ghosts, movies about ghosts, and people even dress up like ghosts – especially around Halloween. The Devil has accomplished his purpose. Many people believe in ghosts – but not in Hell.

But God clearly tells us that *human spirits do not wander the earth as ghosts:*

> "It is appointed unto men once to die, but after this the judgment" (Hebrews 9:27).

That verse plainly says that you die, and then you go to the judgment. You *don't* stay on earth as a ghost. When you're dead, you go to the judgment! And Jesus told us that the place of judgment is Hell:

> "And these shall go away into everlasting punishment..." (Matthew 25:46).

27

> "Depart from me, ye cursed, into everlasting fire, prepared for the devil and his angels" (Matthew 25:41).

We have an example of this in the sixteenth chapter of Luke, where Jesus said:

> "The rich man also died, and was buried; And in hell he lift up his eyes, being in torments..." (Luke 16:22-23).

He died. His body was buried. His soul went directly to Hell! And that is where *you* are going to go unless you experience conversion. *You* will die. *Your* body will be buried. *Your* soul will go directly to Hell!

The Bible says, "How shall we escape, if we neglect so great salvation?" (Hebrews 2:3). How *are* you going to escape from the judgment of God for your sins? How *are* you going to escape from Hell?

You will be everlastingly punished for your sins unless you are converted. Jesus said:

> "Except ye be converted....ye shall not enter into the kingdom of heaven" (Matthew 18:3).

The Devil and the demons want to keep you in the dark about Hell. They don't want you to believe in Hell. That's the first reason they pretend to be ghosts.

Demons Pretend to Be Ghosts To Make People Think There is No Heaven to be Gained

You see, if human souls wander around on earth, then there is no place called Heaven that you can go to – if you are prepared – if you are converted. Remember that Jesus said:

> "Except ye be converted....ye shall not enter into the kingdom of heaven" (Matthew 18:3).

The demons want to keep you from being converted - so they don't want you to think about Heaven. They don't want you to think about how to get there. *That's the second reason they pretend to be ghosts. They don't want you to think about Heaven.*

28

Now the Bible tells us that a converted person goes *directly* to Heaven when he dies:

> "We are confident, I say, and willing rather to be absent
> from the body, and to be present with the Lord"
> (II Corinthians 5:8).

That verse makes it very simple: "Absent from the body – present with the Lord." There is *no* period in between where you walk around on earth as a ghost. No! If you are a real Christian: "Absent from the body - present with the Lord." True Christians go immediately to Heaven when they die.

Can we be *sure* of that? *You bet.* In the sixteenth chapter of Luke Jesus told about a beggar, who was a real Christian:

> "And it came to pass, that the beggar died, and was
> carried by the angels into Abraham's bosom [which is
> another name for Heaven]" (Luke 16:22).

This man was a real Christian. He died and was instantly carried into Heaven by angels! "Absent from the body – present with the Lord." Simple!

But the Devil and the demons don't want you to think about Heaven. Did you ever see a theme park that had anything about Heaven in it? They *could* do that – at Disneyland or Knott's Berry Farm - and it would be *very* interesting – but they *don't!* At both of these amusement parks there are several rides which have ghosts connected with them. And they both have a strong emphasis on ghosts around Halloween. *But neither one of these parks have anything to say about Heaven at all.* Why? Because the Devil is the god of this world (ref. II Corinthians 4:4). God has relegated our sinful world to Satan during this age. He has allowed Satan and demons to control this present world. And the Devil and his demons do not want you to think about Heaven. They want you to keep your mind *only* on this life. They want you to think *only* about this world. That's why they tell you that you're going to come back to *this* world – as a ghost!

But remember that the demons are liars – and they want to destroy you. That's why they want you to think about ghosts. That's why they want you to think that your soul will come back to haunt the earth – or to be reincarnated. *Yes, the demons also teach*

29

reincarnation – for the same reason – to keep you from thinking about Heaven or Hell!

The Bible says, "Resist the devil, and he will flee from you" (James 4:7). You must *resist* the demonic idea that you will come back to this earth as a ghost when you die. *That will not happen!* The truth is that you will either go to Heaven or Hell *immediately after you die.* And whether you go to Heaven or Hell depends completely on what you do with Jesus Christ right now - while you are alive.

Demons Pretending to be Ghosts Have Nothing to Say That Will Help Anyone

I have known people who went to seances. They had "mediums" tell them what the "ghosts" of dead relatives said. There is a séance near the end of that movie, "The Others," I am told. But the ghosts that speak in these seances are really demons. And they have nothing to say that will do you any good.

The demon that spoke to Eliphaz, as described in the fourth chapter of Job, did not help anyone. The demon's message did not help Eliphaz, and it did not help Job. Dr. John F. Walvoord's *Bible Knowledge Commentary* (Victor Books, 1985) points out that the message of the demon pictured "God as unconcerned about man" (comment on Job 4:17-21). That is an outright lie! The demon gave a twisted, false message about God to Eliphaz and confused him. That's why the Bible says:

> "Regard not them that have familiar spirits, neither seek after wizards, to be defiled by them: I am the Lord your God" (Leviticus 19:31).

If you want to know the truth, you have to read the Bible! That's the reason you need to attend Sunday School and church. You need to learn the Bible! It's time for you to find out what *God* says in His Word, instead of what some demon says!

> "We have also a more sure word of prophecy [the Bible], whereunto ye do well that ye take heed [pay attention], as unto a light that shineth in a dark place" (II Peter 1:19).

The Bible is more certain than any voice you could hear – from an angel, or a demon! The Bible *alone* is the sure Word of God. It is like a light shining in a dark place.

> "The law of the Lord [the Bible] is perfect, converting the soul: the testimony of the Lord is sure, making wise the simple...More to be desired are they than gold, yea, than much fine gold..." (Psalm 19:7,10).

Only the Bible can lead you into a real Christian conversion. Only the Bible can give you the wisdom you need. That's why the Bible is more valuable than a pile of gold! Only the Bible can show you how to be saved! *You can't find out any other way!*

Halloween – The Devil's Birthday

Dr. D. A. Waite has written a pamphlet titled "Halloween – The Devil's Birthday." Here is an extended quotation from it concerning the demonic origin of this "holiday":

> Halloween, as we know it, originated in Europe... we Americans continued that fall festival of pumpkin faces...and "trick or treating." The truth is, it was brought over from the Satanic Druid culture of the Celts.
> It's on Halloween...that the witch covens have their great annual worship service and offer a blood sacrifice to Satan. All through the year the Satanists sacrifice cats, dogs, and other animals; but on this special day they offer a human being - one of their own children - which they select for this ghoulish murder! This is shocking! It's the Devil's birthday.
> The ancient Celtic empire extended to France, England, and Ireland...The folklore of early Ireland depicts Druids as a priesthood, offering human sacrifices. One of the chief Druid doctrines which is prevalent today, [was the belief] that men's souls do not perish but transmigrate after death...This is a very serious Satanic [belief]. Many people today believe in the transmigration of souls. We hear them interviewed on radio and television shows (D. A. Waite, Th.D., Ph.D., *Halloween – the Devil's Birthday,* Southwest Radio Church, P.O. Box 100, Bethany, OK 73008).

31

I recently heard two different women on "Larry King Live" say they contact the souls of dead people. They are practicing the Druid custom Dr. Waite spoke about. They believe that our souls roam the earth after we die, rather than going directly to Heaven or Hell, as the Bible teaches.

Dr. Waite said:

> The Druids were Satanic to the core in their worship and pagan practices. Halloween is a Druid holiday that we in America have received from Satanic paganism...The Druid priests believed that on Halloween "Samhain, Lord of Death," called together the wicked spirits [or souls] that within the last 12 months had [died], and allowed them to inhabit the bodies of animals (ibid.).

Dr. Waite tells us that the idea of ghosts wandering around at Halloween came to us directly from the Satan-worship of the Druids.

And there is a great interest in ghosts today. We can tell from the Halloween horror movies that young people flocked to see in 2001, "From Hell," "Vampire Hunter," "The Nightmare Before Christmas," "The Others" and "Thirteen Ghosts." I hope you don't see videos of these movies! They are Satanic!

Disneyland advertises "Haunted Mansion Holiday! Creepy, kooky characters have left no tombstone unturned, [a] spooky experience." Knott's Berry Farm has become "Knott's Scary Farm," full of Halloween ghosts and witches. "The Haunted Queen Mary" [an ocean liner moored in Long Beach, California] presents its seventh annual "Terror Fest" with "seven horrifying mazes!" Sea World and Six Flags Magic Mountain have "ghost shows," and "Frankenstein," the 1931 horror movie starring Boris Karloff, was shown at the Alex Theatre in Glendale, California. All of this Halloween activity focuses people's minds on death and darkness, and on ghosts.

The Bible teaches that there are no real ghosts. What *seem* to be ghosts are really demons – under the control of Satan. Demons *pretend* to be ghosts walking around on earth, to make people think that there is no Heaven or Hell after death. These demons want you to think that your soul will stay on earth, floating around in the air after you die. But the Bible teaches that you will go *directly* to

Heaven or Hell. The Scriptures clearly tell us that all of this emphasis on ghosts is from the Devil and his demons.

Now, I want us to think about how God told us to deal with Halloween across the ages, in each dispensation.

In the Last Dispensation, God's People Were Told Not to Have Anything To Do With Witchcraft or the Demonic

In the last dispensation God was dealing with the world through the nation of Israel. And God told His people to have nothing to do with witchcraft, "ghosts," or demons:

> "There shall not be found among you any one that...useth divination, or an observer of times [an astrologer], or an enchanter [a sorcerer], or a witch, Or a charmer [one who casts spells], or a consulter with familiar spirits [a medium], or a wizard [a spiritist], or a necromancer [one who consults the dead]. For all that do these things are an abomination unto [hated by] the Lord..." (Deuteronomy 18:10-12).

Again, the Old Testament says:

> "Regard not them that have familiar spirits [mediums], neither seek after wizards [spiritists], to be defiled by them: I am the Lord" (Leviticus 19:31).

Mediums and spiritists are people who contact "ghosts," which are really demons. These mediums and spiritists bring back messages which they claim are from "the dead" – but are really from the demons. "The Sixth Sense" was a movie about a little boy who contacted evil spirits pretending to be ghosts. All of this is evil and Satanic. And God told His people to have nothing to do with it. You should be in church instead of playing with demons! You should be in church *every* Sunday. Let fools in the world run after the demons of Halloween! You be in church! You come to Christ! Only Christ can give you eternal life! Peter said, "Lord, to whom shall we go? Thou hast the words of eternal life" (John 6:68).

No one but Jesus Christ can give you eternal life and cleanse your sin by His Blood. Jesus said:

33

"I am the way, the truth, and the life: *no man cometh unto the Father, but by me*" (John 14:6).

And that's why the Bahai religion is *wrong*. Bahai teaches that all religions have the same origin, and that all religions will one day be united together. Actually this is the religion of the Antichrist. What's wrong with it? Bahai says that Buddha, Moses, and Jesus are on the same level as Mohammed – as the founders of religions. That is a demonic lie! Jesus Christ is *not* on the same level as Moses or Buddha, or Mohammed! *Jesus Christ is the Lord of history, the Second Person of the Godhead – the only Redeemer of mankind!* Jesus said, "No man cometh unto the Father but by me" (John 14:6).

"Neither is there salvation in any other: for there is none other name under heaven given among men, whereby we must be saved" (Acts 4:12).

In This Present Dispensation, Early Christians Got Rid of their Occult Books and Turned Away From Demonic Practices

These Christians lived at the very beginning of this dispensation, in the first century. They turned away from their pagan beliefs, and turned fully to Jesus Christ. The Bible tells us,

"And many that believed came, and confessed, and shewed their deeds. Many of them also which used curious arts [practiced magic] brought their books together, and burned them before all men..." (Acts 19:18-19).

These people turned away from their sins. They didn't just *talk* about becoming Christians – they actually turned *away* from their sinful way of life – and they turned *to* Christ. That's what happens when a person is truly *converted* to Christ. The Greek word translated "convert" is "strepho." It means "to turn." To be converted, you have to turn - you turn *away* from the sinful world – and you turn *to* Jesus Christ.

It isn't enough to believe in Christ mentally. That won't save you. The demons believe mentally – but they are lost. Mental belief

34

never saved anyone from judgment. There must be a turning of your heart – *from* sin *to* Christ. The Bible tells us that the early Christians

> "turned to God from idols to serve the living and true God" (I Thessalonians 1:9).

Talking With the Dead

Added to the Halloween madness we see in America today is the growing popularity of communication with the "dead." I heard two women, on two separate telecasts of "Larry King Live," say that they could call the dead back and have conversations with them. These people are mediums. The Bible says that they have a "familiar spirit." The "familiar spirit" is actually a demon, not a ghost. The demon comes and pretends to be a ghost. Demons impersonate ghosts to deceive people into thinking there is no Heaven or Hell after death. These demons beguile people into believing that their souls will wander the earth, rather than going directly into the flames of Hell, as God's Word tells us.

We can learn a great deal about demons and mediums from I Samuel, chapter twenty-eight. Everyone who has an interest in this subject should study this passage of Scripture carefully. There are three main lessons in this chapter.

The first thing we learn is that King Saul disobeyed God by trying to contact the "ghost" of the prophet Samuel. In verse three we read:

> "Saul had put away those that had familiar spirits [mediums], and the wizards, out of the land" (I Samuel 28:3).

Dr. Charles C. Ryrie comments, "In obedience to the law, Saul had removed those who practiced spiritism" (*Ryrie Study Bible*, note on I Samuel 28:3). In Leviticus 20:6; Leviticus 19:31; Deuteronomy 18:11-12, and many other passages of Scripture, God had warned the people not to consult mediums, and not to try to speak with the dead.

But King Saul rebelled against God because he was very afraid. The armies of his enemies, the Philistines, far outnumbered his own men. He was afraid that he might lose the battle. He wanted to know ahead of time what would happen. This fear drove him to seek out one of the mediums he had previously driven from the land of Israel.

Fear is one of the tools of the Devil. If you are afraid of something, the Devil can use it to ensnare you and destroy you. That's how Satan keeps many people from being converted. They are afraid of what might happen if they became true Christians.

The Devil puts thoughts of fear into their minds. They think, "Why, if I went to *that* church, I would lose my friends" (or, "I would lose my fun," etc.). Satan makes them afraid that they will miss out on something good if they go to church and become real Christians. And through that fear, Satan destroys them. That's what the Devil did to King Saul!

King Saul's Disobedience

Deliberate disobedience to God will bring judgment. The Bible says:

> "He, that being often reproved hardeneth his neck, shall
> suddenly be destroyed, and that without remedy"
> (Proverbs 29:1).

You cannot keep living in sin and rebellion without experiencing the judgment of God sooner or later.

That's what happened to King Saul. He sinned – and then he sinned again – and then he sinned again – and again – and again. He thought he was getting away with it. He thought, "God doesn't see. God doesn't know. God won't judge me." But he was *wrong!* The Bible says:

> "Be not deceived: God is not mocked: for whatsoever a
> man soweth, that shall he also reap" (Galatians 6:7).

God finally judged Saul. God cut him off, and never spoke to him again. That's called "the unpardonable sin." It means that you can't be saved. It's too late. God gives up on you and no longer speaks to your heart! That happened to Pharaoh in the time of Moses. That happened to Judas when he betrayed Christ. That happened to King Saul, in the book of I Samuel.

That's why you must be converted and become a true Christian while God is still calling you.

36

The Witch Was Afraid

Think of the fear experienced by the witch of Endor when she saw Samuel:

> "Then said the woman, Whom shall I bring up unto thee? And he said, Bring me up Samuel. And when the woman saw Samuel, she cried with a loud voice..." (I Samuel 28:11-12).

Dr. Merrill F. Unger, late professor of Old Testament studies at Dallas Theological Seminary, gave these comments on the passage:

> Saul asked that Samuel be brought up, that is, from the realm of the spirits, because he knew that there was none like the venerable prophet and judge who knew God's mind and future events so well. The woman doubtlessly began her customary preparations for her control [demon] to take over, entering into a trancelike state to be used by her control or divining demon, who would then proceed to impersonate the person called for.
>
> The startling thing, however, was that the usual occult procedure was abruptly cut short by the sudden and totally unexpected appearance of the spirit of Samuel. Transfixed with terror, the woman screamed out with shock as she [saw] that God had stepped in. By God's power and special permission, Samuel's actual spirit was presented to pronounce final doom upon Saul.
>
> *The medium's terrified conduct at the appearance of a real spirit of a deceased person constitutes a complete scriptural disclosure of the fraudulency of all spiritistic mediumship.* The woman, to be sure, had the power to communicate with wicked spirits. Such deceiving demons represent themselves to their mediums, and through them to their clients, as the spirits of the departed dead. But actually their messages do not [come] from the deceased at all, but from themselves as lying spirits who cleverly impersonate the dead.

The woman's divining demon had nothing whatever to do with Samuel's sudden appearance. She and her spirit accomplice were completely sidetracked. God stepped in and brought up Samuel, who pronounced doom upon Saul. When the medium was exposed and her craft was laid bare as a fraud by her unseemly fright at the appearance of Samuel, the whole proceeding quickly passed over to a conversation between Samuel and Saul (Merrill F. Unger, Ph.D., Th.D., *Unger's Commentary on the Old Testament*, Volume I, Moody Press, 1981, p. 405).

The case of Samuel is actually a strong argument *against* communication with the dead – because it shows that demons enter mediums and pretend to be "ghosts." Two other comments should be made on this point.

1. First, we are literally told that this woman had "a familiar spirit" (I Samuel 28:7). Dr. Murphy Lum, a friend of mine who is an Old Testament scholar, points out that this refers to a spirit (demon) who is familiar to the medium. The medium has "called" the spirit so often that she becomes "familiar" with it.

2. Second, Samuel's spirit coming back from the dead is a one-time event. John MacArthur, though wrong on some things, was right to point out "There is no other such miracle as this in all of Scripture" (*MacArthur Study Bible*, note on I Samuel 28:13). *In no other instance did the dead actually come back to speak to the living.* Therefore, we conclude that every time a so-called "ghost" appears, or someone says they have contacted the dead, the spirit they spoke to is always a demon.

A Description of Demonization

The witch of Endor was frightened when Samuel came to her because no dead person had ever done that before. She had always been indwelt by a demon. Dr. John Nevius, in his classic book *Demon Possession and Allied Themes* (Revell, 1894), gives the following narrative of a Pacific Island medium becoming possessed, which is undoubtedly quite similar to the way the witch of Endor received her "familiar spirit."

> In a few minutes he trembles, slight twitchings of face and limbs come on which increase to strong convulsions with swelling of the veins, murmurs and sobs. Now, the [spirit] has entered him; with eyes rolling and protruding, unnatural voice, pale face and livid lips, sweat streaming from every pore, and the whole aspect of a furious madman, he gives the divine answer, and then the symptoms subsiding, he looks around with a vacant stare, and the deity returns to the land of spirits. (Nevius, ibid., p. 155).

Seek Those Things Above!

Your goal in life is not to learn the future from a dead person's supposed "ghost," or from fortune telling, or from any other occult source.

The Bible tells us exactly what the goal of your life ought to be:

> "If ye then be risen with Christ, seek those things which are above, where Christ sitteth on the right hand of God. Set your affection on things above, not on things on the earth" (Colossians 3:1-2).

Fortune telling, spiritism, astrology, and all forms of magic are from beneath, from this sinful world. "Seek those things which are above, where Christ sitteth on the right hand of God. Set your affection on things above, not on things on the earth" (Colossians 3:2).

A Noose Around Our Necks!

Satanic activities are closing around our throats like a noose. Here is a *Los Angeles Daily News* story which illustrates that point:

Halloween noose act kills boy, 14

SPARTA, Mich. – A 14-year-old boy trying to make his role in a haunted hayride scarier accidentally hanged himself in front of a group of people who thought he was acting. On the ride route at Alpine Ridge Farms, Caleb Rebh was in a scene including a skeleton hanging by a noose in a nearby tree. His mother, Kathy Rebh, said he apparently replace the skeleton with himself to make the scene scarier. Caleb double-knotted the noose loosely around his neck but, when he let go of the rope, he apparently was not heavy enough to prevent the branch from whipping back up and choking him, his mother said. When he started scrambling to get the rope off his neck, fellow hayride workers seemed to think he was acting, she said. (*Los Angeles Daily News*, October 23, 2001, p. 7).

What a horrible tragedy! Yet the involvement of many people with various forms of the occult is proving to be just as great a disaster to our nation.

When the World Trade Center and the Pentagon were terrorized by demonized Muslims on September 11, it was only a further step in the Satanic destruction of America. *We have already opened the door through the occult for our nation to be strangled by Satan and his demons, even without the Muslims as our enemies.*

Our only hope is to turn fully to Christ for salvation, and get into a Bible believing church every Sunday. As America continues to fall prey to demons that is the only safe thing to do!

CHAPTER 3
WHY JOHN WALKER LINDH
JOINED THE MUSLIMS
TO FIGHT THE U.S.A.

Columnist David Limbaugh is the brother of Rush Limbaugh. He reports that *Christmas* is now coming under attack.

> A Frederick County school employee was prohibited from passing out Christmas cards at school because "it may not be a legally protected right on a public school campus."
>
> A Pennsylvania fourth grader was stopped from mailing Christmas cards to classmates.
>
> Two Minnesota middle-schoolers got in trouble for wearing red and green scarves in a Christmas skit and for saying "Merry Christmas" to the audience at the end. (You heard me right – they got disciplined for this!).
>
> Two Massachusetts high school students were forbidden from creating cards saying "Merry Christmas" or depicting a Nativity scene.
>
> An Oregon high school superintendent required removal of Christian but not secular decorations from students' lockers.
>
> A Georgia school board, after being threatened with a suit by the ACLU, deleted the word "Christmas" from the school calendar (worldnetdaily.com, December 20, 2001).

Limbaugh added, "Notice that all of these involve public repression of voluntary student action. You can dress them up in noble-sounding civil rights language or the enlightened [words] of multiculturalism and pluralism, but the bottom line remains: Expressions of Christianity are becoming increasingly taboo in polite American society today" (ibid).

We are in dark times when a Baptist minister, Rev. Ron Sims, joins the attack against saying "Merry Christmas." These are strange days of apostasy – when the Catholic League has more common sense than this Baptist minister.

King County Executive Rev. Ron Sims sent a memo to employees telling them to say "Happy Holidays" or "Holiday Greetings." But he banned the traditional greeting, "Merry Christmas."

Not long ago everyone said "Merry Christmas" and no one thought anything about it. Now it was against policy for a civil service employee to use this cheerful greeting in Seattle, Washington's King County.

Pastor Maynard Sargent of the Salvation Army was upset about the "politically correct" change forced on county employees by Rev. Sims. The Salvation Army pastor "longs for those days when you said what was on your mind and in your heart [as a Christian]" (www.komotv.com/stories; December 11, 2001).

"The Catholic League in New York was none too happy when it heard of [Rev.] Sims' memo. The League sent out its own memo criticizing the King County mandate" (ibid).

"On December 10, the Catholic League issued a news release criticizing a November 14 memo by [Rev.] Ron Sims, the King County Executive in Washington State, that warned county employees not to say 'Merry Christmas.' Sims has now reversed himself, saying that it is okay to say 'Merry Christmas' and 'Happy Hanukkah.' However, Sims, and his chief of staff, Tim Ceis, are now saying that the 'intent' of the initial memo was never to ban these words" [?]. (Actually, they "waffled" under pressure from the Catholic League).

Catholic League president William Donohue commented as follows:

> We are delighted that freedom of speech has been restored to the employees of King County, Washington. The county executive, Ron Sims, wants us to believe that it was his "intent" all along to allow freedom of speech. But the Baptist minister is being disingenuous [dishonest]. What he explicitly said was that "any holiday recognition or celebration should be religion-neutral." He then cited as examples, "Happy Holidays" and "Holiday Greetings." In his latest memo he now says, "I believe its intent [the initial memo] was to ask all of you to remember to be culturally sensitive..."

Whenever someone says of his own words, "I believe its intent was," it's a sure bet he's engaged in spin control. *Sims knows exactly what he meant and what he meant was to censor the speech of county employees. But he got nailed and had to back off.* So now he's sympathetically interpreting his own memo thinking he's fooled us. That is why he unleashed his attack dog, Tim Ceis, to say that the Catholic League's response to the gag rule was "absurd." What's absurd is that he actually thinks someone will believe him.

We can't help commenting on the noticeable absence of the ACLU in this fracas. That's because the champions of free speech are too busy trying to ban kids from singing "Silent Night" in the schools. (www.catholicleague.org).

These are evil days of apostasy and compromise, with a secular, Christ-hating society, led by the ACLU, and traitors like "Rev." Sims, trying to take away our constitutional freedom of speech and freedom of religious expression. Although I disagree with the Catholicism of the League, I am thankful that they had the guts to stand against this wickedness, and keep the right to say "Merry Christmas" for all Americans!

We cannot expect the Roman Catholic Church to save us from these attacks, however. They have been greatly weakened by the scandals that have surfaced regarding pedophile priests. Even without that, they don't have a message that can save our nation or our way of life.

The Story of John Walker Lindh

One of the great tragedies of the past several months was what happened to a twenty-year-old American boy, who left his wealthy home in Marin County near San Francisco and joined the Taliban, the terrorist group in Afghanistan. This young man became a soldier of Allah, and fought alongside Muslim radicals against everything that our nation stands for. I will trace his pilgrimage from middle class America to fanatical Islam. I will try my best to help you learn several important truths from his story.

How did John Walker Lindh become transformed into a radical Muslim zealot and a servant of Osama bin Laden in his war against America? *Time* magazine had a detailed story on Lindh, titled "The Taliban Next Door." *Time* asks:

> At 16, John Walker [Lindh] was a quiet California kid. At 20, he was a Taliban warrior. How did he get from Marin County to Mazar-i-Sharif? (*Time*, December 17, 2001, p. 36).

The steps he took in converting to the Muslim religion were reported in *Newsweek* magazine (December 13, 2001, p. 5). The *Newsweek* article tells us that he

> ...can be at least partly understood as a product of...a reaction against – the culture and mores of a certain time and place. He was born in 1981, a year after the end of the so-called Me Decade that gave rise to a host of self-improvement and self-realization fads. His adolescent years were spent in Marin County, north of San Francisco. Marin County has been gently mocked by the cartoon strip "Doonesbury" as the epicenter of the self-esteem movement, a land of hot tubs, Rolfing and est, a bastion of moral relativism where divorces were for a time listed alongside marriages in the newspaper. Walker was named John after John Lennon, the Beatle. His father says he was not bothered when his two sons rejected the "strict Catholic manner" of his own upbringing. His mother was a child of the '60s who dabbled in Buddhism and home-schooled John for a time. He was sent to an elite alternative high school where students were allowed to shape their own studies and had to check in with their teacher only once a week.
> Walker discovered his passion for Islam online, after sampling other possibilities. At the age of 14, under the handle "doodoo," he was visiting Web sites for hip-hop music with particularly crude raps on sex and violence. In one e-mail posting, he scorned a critic of hip-hop as a "worthless d—rider." In one e-mail at the height of his fascination with hip-hop, he appeared to pose as an African American, writing, "Our blackness should not make white people hate us." But

44

as he got older, he veered to a very different direction. He began visiting Islamic Web sites, asking questions like, "Is it all right to watch cartoons on TV or in the movies?" His family says that the turning point [came] at the age of 16 when he read "The Autobiography of Malcolm X," which describes the conversion to Islam of the famous black militant...young Walker soon became pretty militant himself...Selling off his hip-hop CD collection on a rap music board, he converted to Islam.

He began wearing Islamic dress, a long white robe and pillbox hat, and calling himself Suleyman. His flowing robes raised eyebrows, even in Marin County, which is deeply tolerant of almost any form of self-expression..."That's not your normal Marin County attire," says a former neighbor...Walker's parents [did not want to call] him "Suleyman" (he remained "John" to them).

At about this time, late 1998, Walker's parents were [divorcing]...Their teenage son became obsessed with memorizing the Quran and the Sharia, Islam's...fixed rules for living.

He Grew to Hate Our Lonely, Hedonistic Way of Life

That *Newsweek* quotation makes it quite clear why John Walker Lindh turned against the modern American way of life. He *hated* the way we live!

He rejected the modern values of American society. He rejected the man he was named after – John Lennon. He rejected the moral and spiritual looseness of his parents. He *totally* rejected his typically weak Hippie-generation father.

Why did he do that? *Newsweek* points out:

Lindh was critical of America as a land that exalted self above all else. Americans were so busy pursuing their personal goals, he said, that they had no time for their families or communities. In the Islamic world, by contrast, he felt cared for by others. *"In the U.S. I feel alone," he said. "Here I feel comfortable and at home"* (*Newsweek*, December 13, 2001, p. 2).

Loneliness! *There you have it!* American young people like John Walker Lindh feel lonely. Their parents aborted or otherwise ruined their brothers and sisters, so there is no real home. With no family life, these kids are alone.

That's what happened to John Walker Lindh. Both parents went their separate ways – so they weren't at home. They had moved him from Maryland to California at ten, so he lost all his childhood friends. His mother rebelled against her Catholic husband and became a Buddhist, so he had no church fellowship. They put him in a liberal school that made Malcolm X a hero and belittled or disregarded Washington, Lincoln or any of the true heroes of America.

They gave John Walker Lindh __nothing__ emotionally or spiritually. They handed him a book about Malcolm X – and then they were surprised that he believed it!

Writing for NBC News, Richard Rodriguez said:

> One suspects a lonely child [of course – after his parents ripped him out of school in Maryland!]...one wonders about the other kids at school, the pot, the sex, the routine chaos of American adolescence, *the empty big house*, the pimpled movies at the mall, the idiot gangs of jocks and goths (msnbc.com/news, December 13, 2001).

Isn't that the way __you__ see America? Doesn't the modern American way of life make you sick at the stomach, like it did John Walker Lindh? Aren't you nauseated by our whole stupid, meaningless way of life? The Bible says, "Professing themselves to be wise, they became fools" (Romans 1:22).

He Rebelled Against the Moral and Spiritual Decadence of his Old Hippie Parents, and Their Generation

I'm older than the Hippies. I'm from the generation *before* the Hippies were born. And all of my life I've hated what most of them believe. I can fully understand why many college-age young people today are against the outdated Hippie way of looking at things.

My two teenage sons and I were watching a TV program on the 100 greatest rock songs. These were voted on by the Hippies themselves. They voted the Beatles as number four, Bob Dylan as number three, Aretha Franklin (of course – always politically correct) as number two, and Mick Jagger and the Rolling Stones as number one ("I Can't Get No Satisfaction" as the number one rock song of all time). As I watched those old video clips of Bob Dylan and Mick Jagger, I remembered how much I hated their music back in the sixties. Mick Jagger and Bob Dylan were singing about drugs and political correctness, and free sex and rebellion. *I knew they were no good then – and I know it now!!! Young people – the Hippie generation has <u>nothing</u> to offer you! Bill Clinton's generation is self-centered, self-righteous and self-willed. They are spiritual degenerates. They are moral relativists. They are rootless materialists. They are baby-murdering abortionists. They are Christ-rejecting, church-rejecting, libertarianists. I hate the Hippie way of life – and I don't blame John Walker Lindh for doing the same thing! Reject the old Hippies! Throw out their way of life! Join a Bible-believing church and become a real Christian!*

If you are a young person reading this book, have you ever wondered why your parents didn't take you to church each Sunday? Have you ever wondered why your parents divorced? Have you ever wondered why your house was *so cold and so lonely?*

I will give you the answers to every one of those questions – it's because your parents were not real Christians! It's as simple as that!

Young person – do you want to get divorced some day? Young person – do you want to grow up and have a cold and lonely house? No? Then you have to join a Bible-preaching church, come to Jesus Christ, and become a *real* Christian!

The Ten Commandments are given in Exodus, chapter twenty. In the Second Commandment, God said:

> "Thou shalt not make unto thee any graven image, or any likeness of any thing that is in heaven above, or that is in the earth beneath, or that is in the water under the earth. Thou shalt not bow down to them nor serve them: for I the Lord thy God am a jealous God, visiting the iniquity of the fathers upon the children unto the third and fourth generation of them that hate me; And shewing mercy unto thousands of them that love me, and keep my commandments" (Exodus 20:4-6).

47

This commandment condemns idolatry, which is the main sin of America. The Hippie generation made idols out of drugs, sex, and libertarianism. They "worshipped and served the creature [the world and themselves] more than the Creator" (Romans 1:25). *The Hippies were worried about saving trees and whales – while they murdered 40 million babies – and left you alone in front of the TV – in an empty, lonely house!*

The Hippies made idols out of trees and whales. They smoked weed and became Hindus and Buddhists and free thinkers. Most of them could handle everything – except zealous Christianity. They wanted any god at all – as long as it wasn't the serious God of the Bible.

And so God "visited the iniquity of the fathers upon the children" (Exodus 20:5). No wonder you're so confused. Your parents didn't go to church regularly and they raised you as an American heathen! Your parents *really* messed you over!

The Case of the Dirty Bomber

Jose Padilla is the young man who was arrested for trying to build a nuclear bomb to destroy one of our cities. *Time* magazine tells us his story:

> Padilla grew up in a small gray-stone apartment building in the predominantly Hispanic Logan Square neighborhood of Chicago...Padilla played basketball in the school yard across the street and attended [the Roman Catholic] St. Sylvester Church with his mother, brother and two sisters...At Darwin (!) Elementary School, school counselor Art Ryder remembers him not as a bully but as a force. "You always got the feeling that he wasn't looking for trouble – but if you started it, he'd finish it. He had eyes that could stare right through you." Growing up in a place racked by gang violence, that fearlessness could be an asset.
>
> In his early teens, Padilla joined the Latin Disciples, a mostly Puerto Rican gang. When he was 14, Padilla and several of his friends assaulted and robbed three men...Padilla was convicted of aggravated battery and armed robbery and went to juvenile detention when he was 18.

48

Padilla went on to rack up a grim...rap sheet of adult crimes..."He was a scary, scary guy with a Yankees cap covering his eyebrows" remembers...Victor Lento, 32.

Padilla and [his girlfriend] found jobs and a mentor in the restaurant's manager, Mohammed Javed, a Pakistani immigrant...When Padilla, who had undoubtedly heard about Islam in prison, began asking him how to convert, Javed says he told Padilla to find a mosque on his own.

And so Padilla began a 10-year odyssey, moving ever closer to radical elements within Islam...

Around the time of his conversion [to Islam], Padilla legally changed his name to Ibrahim...He started wearing a red-and-white kaffiyeh, or headdress...In 1998, Padilla suddenly left his wife and moved to Egypt, telling his acquaintances...that he was going to learn Arabic. He [then] moved to Pakistan and Afghanistan...In the spring of this year, he met Abu Zubaydah for the first time – and allegedly made his nuclear bomb pitch.

In March Abu Zubaydah was captured in Pakistan. A month later, he hinted to his FBI and CIA interrogators that he had talked to people who wanted to put together a dirty bomb, says a U.S. official. He provided no details, but agents started comparing intelligence...Out popped Padilla's name, the official says...The chase was on...After Padilla deplaned in Chicago, customs officials pulled him aside...

On Monday morning, [Attorney General John] Ashcroft held his hastily arranged press conference in Moscow. He...described Padilla as a "known terrorist" pursuing an "unfolding terrorist plot" – leaving the impression that other bombers were still at large. He said...that a dirty bomb "can cause mass death and injury"... (*Time* magazine, June 24, 2002, pp. 28-32).

This is the story of yet another American boy who rejected our way of life to become a dirty nuclear bomber for the Muslim terrorists. Like John Walker Lindh, he turned his back on our way of life and joined the militant forces of Allah. He had given up on America, and had turned away from Christianity, as he had experienced it in the Catholic Church.

A growing number of young people are now turning to Islam. *U.S. News and World Report* says, "Hundreds of Americans have followed the path to Jihad [Muslim holy war]" (*U.S. News and World Report,* June 10, 2002, p. 17).

John Walker Lindh, Jose Padilla, And Others Who Join Islam, Have Made the Wrong Choice

You must leave the hedonistic American pathway to find true happiness. But where do you turn when you leave this way of life? John Walker Lindh and Jose Padilla turned to the misleading faith of the Muslims. They turned to their false god – Allah. They turned to their Satanic book – the Koran.

The *correct* answer to life's great questions cannot be found in Islam. The correct answer is found *only* in Jesus Christ – and in a Bible-believing church! *There is no other answer to the problems you face in life!* You must come to Jesus Christ and be saved. Jesus Christ is the answer to your unhappiness and loneliness.

Now, how do you come to Christ? *First,* you must go to a good church every single Sunday – to hear the gospel. That is critical – if you want to become a real Christian.

Secondly, you must go through the inner turmoil and struggle of conversion. You must inwardly come to the place where you distrust your own mind, and hate your own sin. You must begin to literally detest your own sinful nature.

Third, you must throw yourself on Jesus for mercy. He has risen from the dead and is now seated on the right hand of God in Heaven. Come to Him. Believe on Him with all your heart. He will save you from sin, Hell, and the grave.

"Believe on the Lord Jesus Christ, and thou shalt be saved" (Acts 16:31).

As the Puritan hymn writer Joseph Hart put it:

The moment a sinner believes,
And trusts in his crucified God,
His pardon at once he receives,
Redemption in full through His Blood.
("The Moment a Sinner Believes" by Joseph Hart, 1712-1768).

When you put the full weight of your belief on Jesus Christ, the Son of God, He will forgive your sins and you will be converted – by Him. It can all happen in a few moments of time if you will throw yourself on the Son of God! Then get into a good, Bible-believing church!

The Raging Nations

Dr. M. R. DeHaan once said:

> We know that the raging of the nations against Christ goes back to Jesus' first coming and will continue till He comes again...The world is against Christ, and if we fully follow Him, we too shall find out that we are not wanted. The nations rage, says David, because they are against Christ, God's anointed one (M. R. DeHaan, M.D., *Coming Events in Prophecy*, Zondervan, 1962, p. 99).

> "...the rulers take counsel together, against the Lord, and against his anointed [Jesus], saying, Let us break their bands asunder, and cast away their cords from us" (Psalm 2:2-3).

And this is exactly what has happened in our time. With a desire to be completely free from God, man has done nearly everything possible to cast out God and live his life in total autonomy – without God or the Bible.

That's the way life is in our country today. Each person is autonomous. Most people live for themselves alone. And this has produced a nation of angry, frustrated, and lonely people.

The main philosophy of our age is humanism. Man has "dethroned" God and placed himself as the lord of life. Humanism is the greatest single error in the thinking of the American people.

"God isn't going to tell *me* what to do! I'll do what *I* think is right!" These ideas come out of humanism. And the two major errors of our time are rooted in this false, man-centered philosophy: the lie that human reason replaces the Bible and the lie of libertarianism.

The Error of Human Reason Replacing the Bible

In the late nineteenth and early twentieth centuries most people turned away from the Bible to their own views. Instead of finding out what God thinks by reading the Bible, they turned to what some other human being thought. People are no longer interested in what God thinks. All they care about is what they, as human beings, think.

Notice that I said this was the major error of the 20th century. *Nearly all other false ideas flow out of this error – the idea that you do not need to know what the Bible says, because you can make up your <u>own</u> mind on everything.* That is pure, raw humanism – and it permeates nearly every part of our society – and our personal lives as well. The Bible predicted this humanistic age:

> "For the time will come when they will not endure sound doctrine, but *after their own lusts* shall they heap to themselves teachers, having itching ears, and they shall turn away their ears from the truth, and shall be turned unto fables" (II Timothy 4:3-4).

This passage of Scripture foretold the fact that humanism would infiltrate the churches in the last days. Humanism is basically the view that man's reason is the source of all knowledge. It is a turning away from the Bible to human reason as the basis of knowledge. Humanism is exactly what was predicted for our time in II Timothy 4:3, "after their own lusts [i.e. according to their own desires] shall they heap to themselves teachers..."

This verse prophesied that people in our day would "not endure sound doctrine" but would turn to their own "lusts." That is, they would turn from the Bible to their own desires and ideas. And that's exactly what they have done – people have turned from God's Word to human reason – to humanism.

Isn't that *precisely* what young people constantly hear from unbelieving professors in their secular high schools and colleges? They hear these teachers belittle the Bible repeatedly. And they hear them give humanist answers to the great questions of life, answers based purely on human reasoning.

I believe that the modern idea of replacing the Bible with human thought is the single greatest error of the 20th century. But humanism did not make our world a better place to live. It literally ruined the world in the 20th century. Humanism was directly responsible for producing Hitler and the Holocaust, Lenin and Stalin and their Communist dictatorships, as well as Mao Tse Tung and Ho Chi Minh, and their brutal regimes. Humanism was the philosophy behind World War I, World War II, and most of the other great wars of the 20th century. Humanism produced a disregard for human life in Nazi Germany. Humanism was behind the U.S. Supreme Court decision to exterminate 40 million children in the Abortion Holocaust. And humanism has produced the break-up of the home and the social isolation experienced by millions in our nation today. Humanism has not helped us. In fact, it has nearly destroyed the Western world.

Many people are lonely today. Most college-age young people experience heartbreaking loneliness. So do older people, because the social fabric of America has largely been destroyed by humanism.

Libertarianism – The Error of Complete Human Autonomy Replacing Church Membership

The word "autonomy" means "without outside control" (*Webster's New Collegiate Dictionary*). "Autonomy" means that you are completely free as an individual, and you must not be restrained from absolute individual freedom by anything – not even God or the church. This view is called, "libertarianism." Dr. Francis Schaeffer pointed out that drugs are the ultimate end of the road in autonomy, because people use drugs to "seek truth inside one's own head" (Francis A. Schaeffer, *How Should We Then Live?*, Revell, 1976, p. 171). Drugs are also used today by people who are so caught up in their own autonomy, or freedom, that they think nothing matters in life except making themselves "feel good."

The exaggerated importance of autonomy in libertarianism has destroyed the home. Each person in a marriage feels that he or she must be "free" of all restraints to do his or her "own thing." Thus, an exaggerated view of autonomy has destroyed the social fabric of the home and real friendships in our society. If you want to stay married, you have to give up some freedom. Just to have close friends requires giving up some personal desires, and being restrained by the wants and desires of another person.

The absolute freedom of libertarianism has produced great, aching loneliness in this generation. The Bible says, "A man that hath friends must shew himself friendly" (Proverbs 18:24). In other

53

words, if you want real, lasting friends you have to give up a little of your own freedom and be kind and dependable toward others. You can't ever have real friends without giving up some measure of freedom – "to do your own thing," as the Hippies put it. If you are always doing your own thing you will always be alone, because no one wants to be close to someone who thinks only about his own personal happiness, without caring about anyone else's feelings. Put it down as a great lesson of life – *if you want to be absolutely free, you will end up absolutely alone. Libertarianism produces loneliness.*

Nietzsche Went Insane!

The German philosopher Friedrich Nietzsche (1844-1900) believed in complete freedom, even from God – total autonomy! He rebelled against his father, who was a Christian pastor, and said, "God is dead." He was the first leading intellectual to say that. He threw off God and the church, and thought that this would make him free. Instead it drove him insane, lost in a swirling mass of despair, alone. Dr. Francis Schaeffer said of him, "I am convinced that when Nietzsche came to Switzerland and went insane...it was because he understood that insanity was the only philosophic answer if the infinite-personal God does not exist" (ibid., p. 180).

One fourth of the American people will experience Alzheimer's disease or some other form of dementia before they die. Psychiatrists are now telling us that much of this mental illness is aggravated and intensified by loneliness – which is the result of complete individual "freedom." Alcoholism and drug abuse are also direct results of the loneliness that comes by pursuing the total autonomy of libertarianism. Absolute autonomy cuts us off from closeness to others – and leaves us vulnerable to the insanity that Nietzsche experienced.

Loneliness can literally drive you to mental illness, despair, and even suicide. What is God's answer to your loneliness? It is the institution of the local church! That's why I repeatedly preach, "Why be lonely? Come home – to church!"

The early Christians show us how the local church can cure loneliness. The Bible says:

> "And they, continuing daily with one accord in the temple, and breaking bread from house to house, did eat their meat with gladness and singleness of heart,

Praising God, and having favour with all the people.
And the Lord added to the church daily such as should be saved" (Acts 2:46-47).

That's what God wants *you* to do! He wants you to become part of a Bible-believing local church! Your loneliness can only be cured by deep involvement in a good church.

Many philosophers have noticed that modern man is filled with what they call "angst" – that is, "a gloomy, often neurotic, feeling of generalized anxiety and depression" (*Webster's New Twentieth Century Dictionary: Unabridged*). Nearly everyone I talk to has "feelings of anxiety and depression" – and these are rooted in deep feelings of loneliness.

These feelings of "angst" have become common among our people because of the extreme emphasis on individual freedom – the libertarianism in our culture. I've just been reading in *Time* magazine about John Walker Lindh, the twenty-year-old boy who left his wealthy Marin County home, converted to Islam, and joined the Muslim "holy war." He saw Osama bin Laden several times, according to the article. This young person was arrested by the U.S. Army while fighting alongside the Muslims against the USA, in the war in Afghanistan (ref. *Time*, December 17, 2001, pp. 36-38).

As I read the *Time* article, I understood fully why this young man turned his back on America and joined the Taliban. He was inspired to convert to Islam by reading *The Autobiography of Malcolm X.* He rejected the whole phony, politically correct, mindless, loose, totally autonomous, libertarian philosophy of America. He also rejected American materialism. *By joining the Taliban, John Walker Lindh was saying, "I reject the American way of life. I reject it so strongly that I will fight against it." Jose Padilla was saying the same thing when he decided to build a "dirty" nuclear bomb to blow up one of our cities.*

John Walker Lindh is not crazy. I disagree with him, but he is *not* insane. Neither is Jose Padilla. *It's the American people who have gone crazy!* In fact, as I read those articles, some of the things these young men say appear more sane than Lindh's parents, or the morally bankrupt Americans of San Francisco's Marin County. Kids like the 20-year-old Lindh used to become Christians through the "Jesus Movement." But that movement turned into soft charismatism, which now has little appeal for energetic young men like John Walker

Lindh and Jose Padilla. I believe there are kids in Marin County, and across America, who are looking for a strong, vigorous Christianity. No wonder our churches are dying. We need churches run by men. Our kids need masculine Christianity. If we don't give it to them, they will look somewhere else – perhaps to Islam. There could well be an explosion of American conversions to the Muslim religion unless American Christians wake up and give our kids a Christianity with guts – that heals their loneliness and gives them a cause to live for and a flag to march under!

I wish I could have had a chance to preach to John Walker Lindh. I wish I could have told him that he was absolutely right to hate the false, materialistic, anything-goes, American way of life. I wish I could have told him that the God of the Bible hates the American humanist way of life as much as he does. I wish I could have said that to John Walker Lindh, and to all the kids who have been cheated by American humanism, "Jesus Christ is the true answer to your search for a better way."

> I am bound for the promised land, I am bound for the promised land;
> O who will come and go with me, I am bound for the promised land.
> ("On Jordan's Stormy Banks" by Samuel Stennett, 1727-1795).

John Walker Lindh and Jose Padilla converted to the Muslim religion. That's fairly easy to do. You grow a beard and pray five times a day, and you are instantly a Muslim. But converting to Biblical Christianity is an *inward* experience. To become a real Christian, you must undergo an inner struggle between your sinful nature and God. You must then experience awakening, which makes you see that you are depraved and sinful and hopeless. Then, you must go through conversion itself – in which you come directly to Jesus Christ. This whole struggle and change is an *inward* conversion – between you and Jesus Christ. Only when you trust Jesus alone are you converted and washed from your sins by His Blood. Jesus said, "Except ye be converted…ye shall not enter into the kingdom of heaven" (Matthew 18:3).

In this chapter we could only touch on two of the major errors of the 20th century – humanism and libertarianism. I am convinced that the free-floating angst – the anxiety, depression and loneliness – of people today can only be overcome by *rejecting outright* the ideas of humanism and libertarianism.

I am asking you to turn away from mere human reason, and turn back to the Bible. I am asking you to turn away from the absolute individual freedom of libertarianism – and come into a Bible-believing church – every Sunday! And then come to Jesus Christ, and be cleansed by His Blood, and saved by His life.

> "The kings of the earth set themselves, and the rulers take counsel together, against the Lord, and against his anointed [Jesus], saying, Let us break their bands asunder, and cast away their cords from us" (Psalm 2:2-3).

They have thrown out the Bible. *They* have cast away the Scriptures – and have embraced human reason. *Instead, you should throw out humanism – and come back to the Bible!*

They have "cast away" the local church and have embraced libertarianist autonomy! *You should throw out libertarianism – and come into a good local church every Sunday!*

They have turned away from Jesus Christ and have bowed to the idols of materialism, drugs and sex. *Instead, you should throw out materialism and come directly to the risen Christ!*

CHAPTER 4
LESSONS FROM THE TERRORIST ATTACK

> "They mocked the messengers of God, and despised his
> words, and misused his prophets, until the wrath of the
> Lord arose against his people, till there was no remedy.
> Therefore he brought upon them the king of the
> Chaldees, who slew their young men with the
> sword..." (II Chronicles 36:16-17).

We have had some very great preachers in the past 125 years,
but we rejected most of them. Spurgeon was rejected and even
censured by the Baptist Union of Great Britain. He withdrew and
became the first independent Baptist. But they rejected great
Spurgeon! They censured him for holding the fundamentals of the
Christian faith! The English-speaking world paid a heavy price for
casting Spurgeon aside. He died in 1892, at the age of 57. His wife
said that the censure contributed to his early death. Twenty-five years
after he died, England and America were both drenched in the blood
of World War I, "They mocked the messengers of God, and despised
his words, and misused his prophets, until the wrath of the Lord arose
against his people, till there was no remedy."

J. Gresham Machen was a Presbyterian who taught at Princeton
Theological Seminary from 1914 until 1929. He took a strong stand
for Bible-believing Christianity and, as a result, left Princeton to form
the more conservative Westminster Theological Seminary in 1929, of
which he became the president. He was charged with insubordination
by the Presbyterian church and was found guilty. They defrocked
him and suspended him from the ministry. He died suddenly at the
age of 56 in 1937. Machen was an outstanding defender of the faith,
but he was rejected. The American people paid a heavy price for
casting Machen aside. Hitler declared war against America in 1941,
four years after his death. "They mocked the messengers of God, and
despised his words, and misused his prophets, until the wrath of the
Lord arose against his people, till there was no remedy."

During this period of time, in the early 20th century, the Southern
Baptist Convention rejected the preaching of J. Frank Norris and John
R. Rice. They were both outstanding men, but they were driven out
of the Southern Baptist Convention because they took a strong stand

against liberalism, and defended the Bible. America paid a heavy price for casting aside Dr. Norris and Dr. Rice. We were plunged into the Korean War shortly after the Southern Baptists rejected them. "They mocked the messengers of God, and despised his words, and misused his prophets, until the wrath of the Lord arose against his people, till there was no remedy."

The same thing happened to two outstanding Methodist preachers during this period as well. Dr. Bob Jones, Sr. and "Fighting Bob" Shuler were forced to leave the Methodist Church. Their preaching was rejected, and they were compelled to separate from the Methodists. America was snared in the jungles of Vietnam a few years later. "They mocked the messengers of God, and despised his words, and misused his prophets, until the wrath of the Lord arose against his people, till there was no remedy."

The First Lesson We Learn from the Recent Attack on America is that Our Nation is Still Rejecting those who Speak the Truth

In the year 2000, the American news media virtually censured Bob Jones University for proclaiming the Protestant message of salvation. The University was attacked by the media for proclaiming the faith of our Baptist and Protestant forefathers.

Tonight I saw this same rejection going on concerning two men who dared to tell the truth about the recent attack on the World Trade Center and the Pentagon. Jerry Falwell was on Pat Robertson's program. He correctly said that "God gave the U.S. what it deserved" for supporting the ACLU, feminists, perversion, and abortion. Falwell said, "God continues to lift the curtain and allow the enemies of America to give us probably what we deserve," as he spoke on Robertson's "700 Club" television program. Robertson replied, "Jerry, that's my feeling. I think we've just seen the antechamber to terror. We haven't even begun to see what they can do to the general population."

While I disagree with Robertson and Falwell on a number of other issues, I believe they were exactly right in calling the terrorist attack a judgment of God on America because of our sins – particularly the "national sin" of America – the wholesale slaughter of 40 million American children through the Abortion Holocaust.

Falwell and Robertson were attacked so strongly for saying this that both of them gave in to the liberal media, and retracted what they had said. What a shame – because they were quite correct Scripturally.

The Second Lesson We Learn from the Terrorist Attack is that Islam is a Bloody Religion of Hatred

Oh, I know that I will be chastized and lectured for saying this, but like Falwell's statement, it is absolutely true.

To be sure, there have been crusades, led by medieval Roman Catholics, but it takes a real stretch of imagination to blame Protestants, or Baptists, for the Crusades! *Across more than 600 years Baptists have never persecuted the Jews, the Arabs, or anyone else. You cannot imagine any Protestant, Baptist, or even a modern Catholic, doing what the Muslim terrorists did to the World Trade Center and the Pentagon on September 11.*

There is no Assembly of God holy war. Suicide bombers do not quote the words of Jesus. Muslim mosques are not burned down in Indonesia by Baptists. Unbelievers are not converted to evangelical churches by the sword!

No, it is quite clear that there is something very basic in Islam that produces violence and terrorism.

The liberal press is trying to pin the blame on U.S. support of Israel. What else is new? They are saying that U.S. support of Israel is what triggered the terrorism, that Islamic "fundamentalists" have been stirred up against us because we support the Jews in Israel. I say, "hogwash!" *Islamic terrorists have been burning Christian churches and forcing Christian children to convert to Islam in Indonesia for years. The war of Muslims against Christians in Indonesia has nothing whatever to do with U.S. support of Israel!* But it *does* have something to do with the Koran, which teaches, "Destroy the infidels." *The burning of Christians in the Sudan, in Africa, the pillaging and raping, the mutilating and terrorism against Sudanese Christians has nothing whatever to do with U.S. support of Israel!* But it does have something to do with the Koran, which teaches, "Destroy the infidels." Attacks on Christians and the burning of churches in the Philippines have nothing to do with U.S. support of Israel either. *The jailing of several Christians in Afghanistan for "possessing Christian literature" had nothing to do with U.S. support of Israel.* The Armenians had been citizens of Turkey for centuries. They were at peace in their country. The Muslims of Turkey used the excuse of World War I to systematically exterminate over one million innocent, peaceful Armenian Christians. *The extermination of the Armenians by the Muslims of Turkey had nothing whatever to do with U.S. support of Israel!* It did have something to do with the Koran, which teaches, "Destroy the infidels."

Raymond Lull was a Christian missionary to Algeria. He was arrested and deported twice for preaching the gospel on the street. He went back a third time at the age of 80. While he was preaching the gospel, the Muslims rose up against him and drove him from the city with stones, leaving him with broken bones, half dead. He died from being stoned the next day. *The murder of Raymond Lull by the Muslims in AD 1315 had nothing to do with U.S. support of Israel! There was no state of Israel and no America in 1315!* But there was the book of Islam, the Koran, which teaches, "Destroy the infidels."

So, the second lesson we learn from the terrorist attack is that Islam is a bloody religion of hatred. To support this point, I now quote an entire article by Don Feder, columnist with the *Boston Herald* (September 13, 2001). I am reproducing it in full:

West must resist reverse crusade

In the wake of the greatest carnage on American soil since the Civil War, our leaders tell us we are now at war with terrorism. Where have they been for the past 30 years? The Arab oil embargo wasn't an act of war? What about the 1982 bombing of the Marine compound in Beirut (241 dead) – or the attack on U.S. embassies in Kenya and Tanzania, the Khobar Towers bombing and the assault on the USS Cole?

If it's war, let us be clear about the nature of the foe and not mistake one head for the hydra. It's not just the enemies' forward units – Osama bin Laden, the Taliban thugs, Hamas and Islamic Jihad.

It's not just the fiends who turned commercial airliners into aerial bombs. It's not just the sanctuary states – Afghanistan, Iran and Libya.

It's also the mullahs who tell deluded youth that martyrdom and murder are shortcuts to Heaven. It's government newspapers in Egypt that accuse Jews of conducting blood rites.

It's the Saudis who wouldn't let U.S. servicemen stationed there during the Gulf War wear crosses, even though they were protecting them. It's the Pakistani regime that sentences "blasphemers" to death for insulting the Prophet.

It's the Arab street where the deaths of thousands of Americans were greeted with jubilation. "Beloved bin Laden," they chanted in the Palestinian city of Nablus.

The fires that erupted in the wreckage of the World Trade Center blaze on many shores. The conflagration isn't confined to the Middle East.

The day before the largest building in Manhattan was reduced to rubble, blood flowed in the streets of the Nigerian city of Jos. In the past year, thousands have died in fighting over attempts of Nigeria's northern states to impose Islamic law.

The latest strife, which left dozens dead and hundreds of home and cars smoldering ruins, began when a Christian woman tried to cross the street where a group of Moslem men had gathered for prayer. Thus is Allah honored.

Reports from Indonesia – where the Laskar Jihad has been engaged in religious cleansing in the Moluccas islands – say as many as 5,800 Christians have been forced to convert to Islam, the women subjected to genital mutilation in the process.

"They said that if we didn't convert to their religion, they would cut our throats," one teen-ager recounted. At least they didn't bury her under tons of debris.

"Central Asia Braces to Fight Islamic Rebels," read a May 3 headline in The New York Times.

The Islamic Movement of Uzbekistan is determined to create a clone of the enlightened regimes in Afghanistan (where piety is proved by demolishing Buddhist statues), the Sudan (run by a gang of Simon Legrees) and Iran – which threatens to give the Dark Ages a bad name.

A story in the Feb. 19 Newsweek ("A Spreading Islamic Fire") observed, "In the occupied West Bank, in devastated Chechnya and embattled Kashmir, in parts of Indonesia and the Philippines...Islamist extremists are on the move and in contact with each other."

The article mentions a map posted on the website of a bin Laden cell in Chechnya that shows Islamic green engulfing the world in this century.

Newsweek quotes a retired Pakistani army officer, now a commander of the Kashmir jihad. "There's the American New World Order and this world order," says Ehsan ul-Haq, pointing to the Koran. "The whole of the globe belongs to Allah, and the whole of Allah's law has to be executed on the globe" – which is accomplished by executing Jewish settlers, Serbs in Macedonia and officeworkers in Manhattan.

America is caught up in a world war. Retaliation is easy; comprehension is harder.

We must understand the nature of the conflict. A creed that uses God to justify its horrors deserves to be treated like any other criminal enterprise. There is no United Methodist Jihad. Suicide bombers don't quote the Talmud. Unbelievers aren't converted to Mormonism by the sword.

What is to be done? Wherever Islam seeks to advance by force, it must be resisted. Wherever Christians, Jews or Hindus are threatened – in Africa, Israel, the Balkans, the Kashmir, East Asia – they must be supported. After almost 1,000 years, the Crusades have resumed. But now it's the West that's besieged.

Mr. Feder's column is excellent, but it has one error. It leads us to believe that the Crusades "besieged" Muslim lands, without reminding us that these Muslim lands were Christian lands not long before. Those Christian lands had been pillaged and torn from the Christians, the women raped, the men murdered, and the children forced to convert to Islam. *The Crusades were an attempt to return these formerly Christian lands to their original religion.* I should add here that the Crusades were carried out by Roman Catholics, not Baptists or Protestants, and the Crusades clearly violated the teachings of Christ against the use of force. *But the Crusades should be seen, in all fairness, as a Catholic attempt to regain land that the Muslims took from them.* Today's "holy war" by the Muslims is an effort to force the West to become Muslim, just as they forced their religion on those who were formerly Christians in the Middle Ages. *Will someone have to do a Crusade to liberate America from Islam in the future?*

If you have the slightest doubt that Islam is a bloody religion of hatred, you should buy a copy of *Their Blood Cries Out* by Dr. Paul Marshall, one of the world's leading authorities on religious persecution, Senior Fellow in Political Theory at the Institute for Christian Studies, Toronto, and Adjunct Fellow at Claremont Institute, California. The book is endorsed by Charles Colson, Luis Palau, Ravi Zacharias, J. I. Packer, Jack Hayford, David Aikman of *Time* magazine, and the Baroness Cox, Deputy Speaker of the House of Lords. The second chapter of Dr. Marshall's book is called "The Advancing of Jihad." Read especially the sections titled, "War Without End" (pp. 19-20) and "Islam's Relentless Crusade" (pp. 20-21). You can order it from Amazon.com or through your local Christian bookstore. Ask for *Their Blood Cries Out*, by Paul Marshall (Word Publishing, 1997), $12.95.

The Voice of the Martyrs also has much material available on Islamic terrorism and the Muslim religion. Write to Voice of the Martyrs, P.O. Box 443, Bartlesville, Oklahoma 74005. Phone (918)337-8015. Dave Hunt offers these books, *Who is This Allah?*, *Facts on Islam, Islam and the Gospel*, and *Behind the Veil – Unmasking Islam* (especially good). You can order these books from Mr. Hunt by phoning (800)937-6638 or by writing The Berean Call, P.O. Box 7019, Bend, Oregon 97708.

The Third Lesson We Learn from the Terrorist Attack is that God Judges Sin

This is very clear throughout the Bible. The verses I quoted earlier in this chapter are worth repeating.

> "But they mocked the messengers of God, and despised his words, and misused his prophets, until the wrath of the Lord arose against his people, till there was no remedy. Therefore he brought upon them the king of the Chaldees, who slew their young men with the sword in the house of their sanctuary, and had no compassion upon young man or maiden, old man, or him that stooped for age: he gave them all into his hand" (II Chronicles 36:16-17).

In 1942 Dr. John R. Rice preached a sermon titled "America Gets Back Her Scrap Iron" (ref. *When Skeletons Come Out of Their Closets*, by John R. Rice, Sword of the Lord, 1943, pp. 45-57). In this sermon Dr. Rice told how America sold millions of pounds of scrap iron to Japan with

> a clear understanding that they were to kill helpless Chinese with them. And now, after murdering something over a million Chinese, mostly innocent non-combatants, women and children who could not help themselves nor fight back [including Dr. Hymers' former pastor's first wife and small daughter], Japan has now begun to kill Americans with our own scrap iron! How wicked, how sinful are the Japanese, to kill armed American soldiers and sailors, instead of killing helpless Chinese as the understanding was when we sold them the scrap iron along with the airplanes, the oil and some of the bombs to do it with! (ibid, p. 45).

Dr. Rice said that nations, as well as individuals, reap what they sow:

> God has a hand in every war. For His own reasons He allows suffering and death and ruin that come when wicked men bring on war...God allowed Japan to bring on war, and *doubtless it was in punishment for our sins* (Dr. John R. Rice, ibid, p. 48).

He cited II Chronicles 36 to show that God sent Nebuchadnezzar, King of Babylon, against Jerusalem. God sent a heathen king against His own people of Judah because of the sins of the leaders, the preachers, and the people. Yes, "God does send heathen armies against the people who know about Him but go on in sin," said Dr. Rice (ibid., p. 49). He went on to say:

> I Chronicles 5:25-26 tells how God "stirred up the spirit of Pul king of Assyria, and the spirit of Tilgath-pilneser king of Assyria" and how he carried away the Reubenites and Gadites and the half-tribe of Manasseh into captivity because of their sins. And the same kind of thing is told in II Kings 21:12-15, in II Kings 24:1-4. And six times in the book of Judges we are told how

God raised up heathen, wicked nations and kings
against His own people Israel because of their sins.
God does punish nations for their sins. God is using
Japan to punish America for our sins (Dr. John R. Rice,
ibid., p. 49).

There can be no question, Biblically or theologically, that Dr.
John R. Rice was correct concerning Pearl Harbor and World War II.
It was a punishment on America for sin. *And there can be no
question that the Muslim attack on the World Trade Center and the
Pentagon was also a judgment from God on our sinful nation!*

Yes, I know, they had Billy Graham speak at the National
Cathedral, and Bill Clinton stood at the door, like a preacher, shaking
everyone's hand as they left. Yes, I know that people put flags on
their cars and on their houses. I know that there were thousands of
prayer meetings all across the nation. I know that millions said, "God
bless America."

But *will* God bless America? I don't know! He may *not.* We
may well have crossed over the line as a nation. It may already be
that "the wrath of the Lord arose against his people, till there was no
remedy" (II Chronicles 36:16). There is another warning in the Bible
that seems to apply to our nation today:

"When your fear cometh as destruction, and your
destruction cometh as a whirlwind; when distress and
anguish come upon you. *Then shall they call upon me,
but I will not answer; they shall seek me early, but
they shall not find me:* For that they hated knowledge,
and did not choose the fear of the Lord: They would
none of my counsel: they despised all my reproof.
Therefore shall they eat of the fruit of their own way,
and be filled with their own devices. For the turning
away of the simple shall slay them, and the prosperity
of fools shall destroy them" (Proverbs 1:27-32).

Murdering the Fatherless

Eliphaz was one of Job's friends who came "to comfort him"
(Job 2:11) when great tragedy struck. He actually gave little comfort
to Job, but wrongly blamed him, because Job was a righteous man.
Yet the *Scofield Bible*'s note on Job 4:1 is correct in saying that

"Eliphaz says many true things, and often rises into eloquence..." One of the true things he said to Job was this:

> "Thou hast sent widows away empty, and the arms of the fatherless have been broken. Therefore snares are round about thee, and sudden fear troubleth thee" (Job 22:9-10).

Although he was wrong to accuse Job of doing this, yet he was right in saying that judgment would fall on those who break the arms of the fatherless. He was right to say that people who do this will have "snares round about [them], and sudden fear trouble [them]" (Job 22:10).

In another place the Bible says:

> "They...murder the fatherless. Yet they say, The Lord shall not see, neither shall the God of Jacob regard it" (Psalm 94:6-7).

That's exactly what many Americans thought after the terrorist attack on the World Trade Center and the Pentagon.

I saw a large group of Hollywood people on television a few nights after September 11, in a patriotic telethon. Hippie country singer Willie Nelson led them in singing "America the Beautiful" and "God Bless America." Clint Eastwood stood behind him singing those songs. So did Jack Nicholson, Sylvester Stallone, Michael Jackson, Muhammad Ali, Liza Minelli, Danny DeVito, Stevie Wonder, and other Hollywood types. Most of them are degenerates who live sinful, pagan lives. These people think they can wave a flag and sing "God Bless America" and everything will be all right. They assume that God will automatically rescue our nation once again if we simply mouth the words of those patriotic songs and wave an American flag! *I don't think so!* God *may* bless America – *but if He does, it won't happen because of a brief show of patriotic fervor by these materialistic, loose living pagans!*

Most of these Hollywood types support abortion on demand, the murder of 40 million babies in the American Holocaust.

> "They...murder the fatherless. Yet they say, The Lord shall not see, neither shall the God of Jacob regard it" (Psalm 94:6-7).

But they are wrong! God *does* see them murder the fatherless! And He is punishing our nation for thinking that He doesn't care about this slaughter any more than they do.

About 3,000 people were killed by the terrorists in the attack on the World Trade Center. My associate, Dr. Cagan, is a statistician. He tells me that is about half the number who die each month, under the abortionist's knife, in New York City. *They murder 20 times as many each year in New York by abortion as were killed in the World Trade Center.*

The liberals and abortionists are all up in arms (as they should be) over 3,000 people who were killed by the terrorists, but they say nothing about the 60,000 who are murdered by abortion each and every year in New York City.

> "They...murder the fatherless. Yet they say, The Lord shall not see, neither shall the God of Jacob regard it" (Psalm 94:6-7).

Notice what God says at the end of this Psalm:

> "And he [God] shall bring upon them their own iniquity, and shall cut them off in their own wickedness" (Psalm 94:23).

I hope this does not apply to America. I hope God will not bring our "own iniquity" upon us. I hope He will not "cut [us] off in [our] own wickedness." *But He may!*

If God doesn't bless America we could be in real trouble in the next few years. Several of these Arab countries will soon have nuclear bombs. They will also have weapons of germ warfare. All of this is known by our government. Will these maniacs unleash a bloody slaughter of atomic warfare and germ warfare against our nation? *Only God can stop them from doing so!* I am not certain that He will.

God Warns Us Not to Harm Fatherless Children

Throughout the Bible, time and again, God warns us not to harm fatherless children. Nowhere is it clearer than in these verses from the Book of Exodus:

"Ye shall not afflict any widow, or *fatherless child.* If thou afflict them in any wise, and they cry at all unto me, I will surely hear their cry; And my wrath shall wax hot, and I will kill you with the sword; and your wives shall be widows, and your children fatherless" (Exodus 22:22-24).

New Yorkers have supported the abortion of 60,000 innocent children every twelve months in their city for the past 29 years. And now God has required the blood of 3,000 of them in payment. That is my belief. I am horrified by the deaths of these 3,000 people at the World Trade Center. *I am also horrified by the murder of 40 million babies in the past twenty-nine years in America!*

These children are often in the 8th and even in the 9th month. They put needles into their brains. They rip off their arms and legs. They disembowel them. They disregard the baby's silent scream!

Most people think that Hitler was judged by God because he killed 6 million Jews by gassing them and burning their bodies in ovens. I agree with them. They are right to think that God judged Hitler for those 6 million murders. But what makes us think that America will escape the judgment of God when we have exterminated nearly seven times as many human beings as Hitler did? If Hitler could not escape the judgment of God, how can we?

God said, in Exodus 22:22-24, that those who harm fatherless children would be thrust into war, with "military invasions," as John MacArthur puts it (MacArthur Study Bible, note on Exodus 22:22). Isn't that precisely what happened in New York on September 11?

Objectively speaking, we should let our minds travel from the world, away from the thoughts of earth-bound people. We should let our minds go up – and out – into another dimension, up into Heaven – where God is. Let us look back to New York from far away in Heaven. Have you ever seen that photograph of the earth which was taken from the moon? Look at it that way – the way God views things. That will help you to understand what God sees. It will help you to be objective.

Objectively, God warns us that He will destroy people in a society which permits the affliction of fatherless children. It's as simple as that.

In his great prophetic sermon, "America Gets Back Her Scrap Iron," Dr. John R. Rice said this, shortly after Pearl Harbor was attacked by the Japanese on December 7, 1941:

> America's sins have brought us the wrath of God. We are suffering for our sins. If we do not repent, our boys will die by hundreds of thousands... (Dr. John R. Rice, "America Gets Back Her Scrap Iron," Sword of the Lord, 1943).

What was true during World War II is still true today. America's sins have brought the wrath of God upon us. We are suffering for our sins. If we do not turn away from sin to Christ, we can expect more judgments from God to strike us.

Don't get me wrong. I am not advocating violence of any kind. That's for the Muslim extremists. No violence should ever be carried out against an abortionist by a Christian, or anyone else with any brains. But if the people of America rose up in a body, abortion would end in our land. We are guilty if we don't stop it.

Many People Think God Will Not See Our Sin of Allowing the Murder of 40 Million Innocent Human Beings

> "They slay...and murder the fatherless. Yet they say, The Lord shall not see, neither shall the God of Jacob regard it" (Psalm 94:6-7).

Many Americans view our situation subjectively. They see things from their own perspective, not from God's perspective. They view things their own way, not as God views them. That's because they do not take the Bible seriously. The only way to escape from subjectivism, and see things from God's viewpoint, is to read the Bible and believe what it says:

> "We have also a more sure word of prophecy [the Bible]; whereunto ye do well that ye take heed, as unto a light that shineth in a dark place..." (II Peter 1:19).

The Bible is "as a light that shineth in a dark place." It shows us what *God* thinks about things! *And the Bible teaches that God thinks abortion is a crime! God says that a nation which condones abortion is doomed. In one way or another, at one time or another, America will ultimately be destroyed unless we rid our land of this evil – this crime against humanity – this stench in the nostrils of God!*

On August 8, 1939, the British statesman Winston Churchill made a fifteen-minute speech on radio to the people of the United States. Hitler was already moving across Europe. Churchill said to his American audience:

> Holiday time, ladies and gentlemen! Holiday time, my friends across the Atlantic!...There is a hush all over Europe, nay, all over the world...If this habit of military dictatorships breaking into other people's lands with bomb and shell and bullet...spreads too widely, we may none of us be able to think of summer holidays for quite a while (Winston S. Churchill, "Holiday Time," August 8, 1939).

"Holiday time" means "vacation time" in England. And that's the way it is, sixty-three years later in America. It's been "vacation time." We have been enjoying a long party – as though the only purpose of life is to play!

People have no time for church. Why, after all, there are so many "fun" things to do on Sundays! After all, it's "Holiday time"! We have no time for God – no time for church!

But *now we are at war with Muslim terrorism. Now we need God.* As Churchill said, "We may none of us be able to think of summer holidays for quite a while."

This is the time for you to get serious with your life. This is the time for you to act like an adult and get your life in order. This is the time for you to stop living as though every Sunday were vacation time. This is the time for you to be in church *every Sunday – and never miss again as long as you live! This is the time for you to turn from your sins to Jesus Christ!*

You have been living your life as though you were constantly on vacation – especially on Sundays. "Wheee! It's vacation Sunday! No time for church or God or Jesus Christ!"

71

But now our country is at war. Vacation time is over. Get into church every Sunday. Come to Jesus Christ, the Son of God. Turn away from your sins and come to Him.

Now is the time for our people to arise and set our nation free. America is at war. Vacation time is over! And let us make no mistake about it – this is a war for the heart and soul of America. No one can set us free but *you* – with the help of God! This is *your* hour. Rise, O citizens of America. Rise up for God and Country. Only you can set our people free again! Only you can overcome the darkness of sin in our land. *I am asking you to take up this cause and make America a godly nation once again.* Come into a Bible-believing local church. Be in church every time the door is open. Come to Jesus Christ, the Son of God. Turn your life over to Him and become a real Christian – *and do it now!*

CHAPTER 5
THE WORLD ON FIRE!

Demonic forces are fiercely attacking our nation. We are facing the danger of thermonuclear war, which is greater now than ever. A recent Hollywood motion picture was titled, "The Sum of All Fears." The ad for the movie said, "27,000 nuclear weapons. One is missing." The film is based on a Tom Clancy novel, and depicts a nuclear attack on Baltimore, Maryland. A recent poll indicates that Americans are extremely frightened about the possibility such an attack. A front page story in the *Los Angeles Times* said:

> **NUCLEAR THREAT IS REAL, EXPERTS WARN**
>
> The former Soviet stockpile is seen as a likely source of weaponry for terrorists. Specialists cite lax security, missing materials and attempted thefts…In the former Soviet Union highly enriched uranium – usable for a nuclear bomb – has disappeared. Among the buyers…Osama bin Laden. Graham T. Allison, Assistant Secretary of Defense under President Clinton, said, *"We have every reason to expect that there will be an act of nuclear terrorism in the next decade – maybe sooner"* (*Los Angeles Times*, November 11, 2001, p. A1).

How long will it be until Los Angeles or some other major city experiences a nuclear explosion? A bombing like that is a distinct possibility in the next few months. This is a frightening and uncertain time in which to live. Our cities could be set on fire by a small nuclear bomb in the trunk of a terrorist's car. The whole world could be set on fire by a nuclear bomb dropped on the oil fields of the Middle East – by some madman bent on destroying civilization.

What will you do when the world is burned? Where will you hide when America goes up in flames? This is not the time to live in sin and miss church. "In times like these, you need a Saviour!" You need to be in church every Sunday in these uncertain days.

Atomic Energy in the Bible

The Bible tells us about atomic energy:

> "The elements shall melt with fervent heat"
> (II Peter 3:10).

The words translated "the elements" in our English Bible are "ta stoicheia" in the original Greek. "Stoicheia" comes from "stoichos" which means "things arranged in a row," like the letters of the alphabet or the elements of nature. Greek Commentator Fritz Reinecker says, "Here it clearly means physical elements...the atomic particles which are the basic structure of nature" (Fritz Reinecker, *A Linguistic Key to the Greek New Testament*, Zondervan, 1980, p. 781).

> "The elements [the atoms] shall melt with fervent heat"
> (II Peter 3:10).

The term "fervent heat" means "a conflagration from internal heat, such as a volcano" (Joseph B. Mayor, *The Epistle of St. Jude and the 2nd Epistle of St. Peter*, Baker, 1965).

> "The elements [the atoms] shall melt with fervent heat
> [like a volcano]" (II Peter 3:10).

And the verse continues:

> "The earth also and the works that are therein shall be
> burned up" (II Peter 3:10b).

Atomic bombs work by the atoms breaking apart. Hydrogen bombs work by the atoms fusing together. The sun is a great hydrogen bomb. An atomic bomb is often used to set off a hydrogen bomb. Both of these weapons work by melting the atoms. It is astonishing that the Bible gave us a clear picture of atomic energy two thousand years ago, in II Peter 3:10.

Dr. M. R. DeHaan said:

These are the amazing words of Almighty God given by the Holy Spirit through the Apostle Peter. These words are true and faithful, spoken by God who cannot lie. A few years ago this description of future destruction by fire might have seemed fantastic to some. Today...it is not only possible, but probable. *Scientists have warned us that man is now in possession of knowledge concerning atomic and cosmic energy which may well result in the destruction of this entire world* (M. R. DeHaan, M.D., *Signs of the Times*, Zondervan, 1951, p. 134).

"The heavens shall pass away with a great noise, and the elements shall melt with fervent heat, the earth also and the works that are therein shall be burned up" (II Peter 3:10).

Atomic Warfare

Dr. DeHaan gave this further comment:

This age will go down in the history of eternity as the atomic age, the age in which man, by God's permission, has solved the secrets of the universe, and now has in his hands a power which, if God would permit it, completely to destroy himself and the world. This secret is not ours alone, but is also in the possession of our enemies. The power to destroy the world is in the hands of wicked men. This is indeed a sobering thought to contemplate. It seems that, with this knowledge, man forever would shun war and outlaw the ravages of war once and for all. It seems that in the light of all we know now about atomic energy, men would realize that our differences *must* be settled by peaceful means, or all must be destroyed together. Such is the depravity of human nature and such is the deception of Satan, however, that man instead of seeking to avert war is pressing it with greater abandon than ever before in all history (ibid.).

Those who know the Bible may scoff and say, "This is all in the future. It doesn't apply to us!" It should be remembered that scoffers like this are spoken of in verses 3-5 of this same chapter in II Peter 3! II Peter 3:10 speaks of the *certainty* of judgment by fire, *not the time.* Although we do not know the exact time, it is absolutely *certain* that

> "The elements shall melt with fervent heat, the earth also and the works that are therein shall be burned up" (II Peter 3:10).

Then, too, Christ warned us of war and turmoil as signs of the end.

> "Ye shall hear of wars and rumours of wars...For nation shall rise against nation, and kingdom against kingdom" (Matthew 24:6-7).

Again, regarding the end-times, Christ said:

> "And great earthquakes shall be in divers places, and famines, and pestilences; and fearful sights and great signs shall there be from heaven" (Luke 21:11).

> "And there shall be signs in the sun, and in the moon, and in the stars; and upon the earth distress of nations, with perplexity; the sea and the waves roaring; Men's hearts failing them for fear, and for looking after those things which are coming on the earth: for the powers of heaven shall be shaken" (Luke 21:25-26).

"Men's hearts failing them for fear...for the powers of heaven shall be shaken." That doesn't sound very happy and promising to me! *It sounds like we could be in for a terrible nuclear war, set off perhaps by Muslim terrorists, possibly bringing in Iraq, Iran, Saudi Arabia, North Korea, and other nations that are now developing the hydrogen bomb, and already possess the atomic bomb!*

A terrorist could bring into one of our cities what is called a "dirty bomb" in the trunk of his car, and press a button. Los Angeles, or some other city, would be contaminated. Radioactive material would be sprayed into the air, and would settle across the city in a fine dust. Anyone breathing or touching this dust would be poisoned by radiation. The poison would rage through their bodies. Their eyes would rot. Their blood vessels would leak. Their internal organs would fail. They would gasp for breath, and choke to death in the vomit of their own blood.

You will not die a pleasant death if that should happen. You will die a horrible, painful death if one of these terrorists explodes a "dirty" atomic bomb near your city. And the poison dust would be deadly for many years to come.

The most dangerous thing about this poisonous dust is that you can't taste it or smell it. You won't be able to tell where it is. And you will be in danger of touching it or breathing it wherever you go.

Remember, this is not science fiction! This is reality! President Bush warned us that Arab leaders are working to get "nuclear weapons right now." They may already have these bombs. This is no joke!

The World on Fire

The Bible says:

> "But the day of the Lord will come as a thief in the night; in the which the heavens shall pass away with a great noise, and the elements shall melt with fervent heat, the earth also and the works that are therein shall be burned up" (II Peter 3:10).

The world on fire! Visions of nuclear war deeply frightened me as a child. In the fourth grade, in Sunnyslope, Arizona, I saw a newsreel about atomic bombs falling on Hiroshima and Nagasaki at the end of World War II. The teacher told us we were all in danger of the Soviet Union dropping such bombs on us. I was *deeply* and *strongly* troubled by all of this during the fifties and sixties.

The younger generation has not, until now, known the terror of the constant threat of nuclear annihilation. It makes my hands sweat tonight, as I write, thinking about the fear of a nuclear holocaust that we lived in constantly during the height of the Cold War, when I was young.

> At 5:30 A.M. on July 16, 1945, a light brighter than a thousand suns illuminated the desert sands of New Mexico. One scientist who was watching wept. "My God," he exclaimed, "we have created hell." From that

day on our world has not been the same. We entered a new era of history – perhaps the last era (Billy Graham, *World Aflame*, Doubleday, 1965, p. xiii).

"My God, we have created hell." That scientist was right. The fire of Hell itself could pour out on our nation and our cities if Satan leads some Arab fanatics to bomb us.

Are you prepared? You say, "What can I do?" The most *important* thing you can do is to be prepared spiritually. The Bible says:

"Prepare to meet thy God" (Amos 4:12).

If you are not prepared to meet God, no other preparation can help you.

Bioterrorism

Time magazine recently featured a news article on bioterrorism (November 5, 2001). It was titled, "What's Next?"

It could be smallpox, botulism or other deadly biological agents. Anthrax is the current focus of the nation's post-September 11 trauma, but it's just one of many potential weapons in bioterrorism's terrible arsenal.

This news article told about bioterrorism through salmonella, drug resistant tuberculosis, and "flesh eating" bacteria. The article continued by telling us,

Even without high-tech delivery systems, a single suicidal terrorist spraying a few drops of smallpox virus – or a liquid solution of Ebola or even plague – in a crowded mall or into the ventilation system of a large building could cause untold harm...Or a terrorist might use...botulism [or] a few drops of cholera bacteria, for example, [to] poison the water tank of an apartment house...Health and Human Services Secretary Tommy Thompson said last week what worries him most is the safety of the nation's food supply, especially of imports...[and] an attack on Americans, if traced back to a state sponsor, could trigger nuclear retaliation. (*Time*, November 5, 2001, pp. 44-45).

78

In other words, terrorism could easily spark World War III – with nuclear bombs going off – here in our cities, the water supply and the food supply poisoned, and thousands infected with smallpox, incurable tuberculosis, or the Black Plague. *This is a frightening time to be alive!* That's why you need to be in church next Sunday – and become a *real* Christian!

We now know that several Arab nations have biological weapons and nuclear devices of terrorism that could destroy our nation within a few hours. This could occur at any moment!

I believe that time is desperately short. What we see in the world today should drive you to repent of sin, turn to Christ, and come into a good church! I am convinced that this is the only way to preserve your life!

President Bush has said that we must be prepared. And *Time* magazine says that even the president is in trouble, "Fighting elusive foes at home and abroad, Bush and his team are feeling the heat" (November 5, 2001, cover). Will America survive? Will our way of life continue? *I don't know.* But I *do* know that Isaac Watts was right when he said,

> Under the shadow of [God's] throne Still may we dwell secure,
> Sufficient is [His] arm alone, And our defense is sure.
>
> O God, our help in ages past, Our hope for years to come,
> Be Thou our guide while life shall last, and our eternal home.
> ("O God, Our Help in Ages Past" by Isaac Watts, 1674-1748).

The Nature of God

Why did these alarming acts suddenly begin happening? Just a few months ago no one was even thinking about terrorism. Why have we quickly and unexpectedly been traumatized by these events? I believe there are several roots of terrorism, several reasons why these horrible acts have occurred.

The Bible teaches that God loves us. But it also teaches that God will not condone sin. He will only put up with sin for so long – and then judgment falls.

God has a special love for Israel and the Jewish people – even today. But God said that He would judge His beloved nation if they "forsook God which made [them]" (Deuteronomy 32:15). There is a principle here that applies to America – because the Bible says, "Righteousness exalteth a nation: but sin is a reproach to *any people*" (Proverbs 14:34). And America, as a nation, has forsaken the God that made us. We have stopped attending church. We have stopped reading the Bible. And the same kinds of judgment that fell on ancient Israel are now falling on us! God said:

> "I will heap mischiefs [disasters] upon them; I will spend mine arrows upon them. They shall be burnt with hunger, and devoured with burning heat, and with bitter destruction: I will also send the teeth of beasts upon them, with the poison of serpents of the dust. The sword without, and terror within, shall destroy both the young man and the virgin, the suckling also with the man of gray hairs" (Deuteronomy 32:23-25).

That's what's happening to America right now! It doesn't matter what some liberal minister, or some weak-kneed evangelical says – that *is* what's happening to America *right now!* And for the *same* reason – our people have forsaken God.

You may *say* you believe in God, but you miss church to serve and worship your *real* god. You work on Sunday because *money* is your *true* god. You miss church to go to a party or a family affair – because your *true* god is *pleasure.* When any little thing comes up, you miss church – because *"any little thing"* is your *true* god – and you do not make the God of the Bible your Lord. Jesus said:

> "Thou shalt love the Lord thy God with all thy heart, and with all thy soul, and with all thy mind. This is the first and great commandment" (Matthew 22:37-38).

And every time you miss church you break the greatest commandment that God ever gave!

Many preachers are afraid to say that. They blame the drug addicts, the ACLU, or the sexual deviants for God's judgment. But they are afraid to tell the truth – the *main* reason for God's judgment is because so-called Christians are not faithful to their local churches. *Killing babies by abortion* and *missing church* are the two biggest national sins of America. I believe one of the reasons that God is judging us is that no-account "Christians" refuse to get into church

Sunday morning, Sunday night, and Wednesday night. If they did that, the churches would be such a mighty force that abortion would end in six months to a year. I blame many evangelicals for God's judgment on this nation. *They are not serious Christians.*

More than one-half of all Southern Baptists attended their church less than one time last year! Think of it! Less than one time! And most of the others came only on Sunday morning. Hardly any of them go on Sunday night. And only a tiny number attend prayer meeting – if the church even has one! *And independent Baptists aren't much better! I believe these so-called Baptists are deeply responsible for bringing the judgment of God on America!*

These spineless "Christians" are rebellious, covetous, lost, and going to Hell. And God says:

> "A fire is kindled in mine anger, and shall burn unto the lowest hell...and set on fire the foundations of the mountains" (Deuteronomy 32:22).

Once the fire of God's judgment is unloosed, it knows no limits in its power. It reaches even to those in Hell! This shows God's eternal judgment of those who oppose Him – especially by lightly missing church on Sunday! Especially by refusing to seek Christ in a true conversion experience!

How is it that a few rag-tag terrorists have this whole nation terrorized, sitting in front of our TVs, biting our fingernails? How could a few scruffy Arabs hold the greatest nation on earth in the grip of terror? The only explanation is that God is judging America for sin. And many preachers are too frightened or self-seeking to say a word! *How could a few crazy Arabs have the greatest nation on earth in their grip if God were not judging us?*

> "How should one chase a thousand, and two put ten thousand to flight, except their Rock [God] had sold them, and the Lord had shut them up?" (Deuteronomy 32:30).

And the only way to escape the judgment of God is to flee to Christ, the Son of God. Come to Christ as quickly as you can! *"Escape for thy life; look not behind thee"* (Genesis 19:17). Get into church *every single* Sunday morning *and* evening. There is *nothing*

81

important enough to make you miss. And then make sure you are converted. Jesus said, "Except a man be born of water and of the Spirit, he cannot enter into the kingdom of God" (John 3:5). Make certain that you are converted, that you have literally come to Jesus Christ, Himself. Make certain beyond a shadow of a doubt that your sin has been cleansed by the Blood of Christ.

Yes, the first root of terrorism is in the very nature of God. "Be not deceived; God is not mocked: for whatsoever a man soweth, that shall he also reap" (Galatians 6:7). God will not let us get away with sin without sending punishment. But God has provided a way to escape judgment – and that way is through Jesus Christ.

The Nature of Man

I just received a fax of a Reuters British-released news story, saying that California governor Gray Davis indicated that he had received "credible" information that the Golden Gate Bridge, or one of the other major California bridges, may be blown up during rush hour. The report went on to say, "Davis said it would be up to commuters to decide whether or not they wanted to cross the bridges during the period in question." At first, the FBI did not confirm this report, but later they said that Governor Davis was correct. The terrorists have the American people desperately frightened.

I said to my wife and boys a month ago, "I'll bet they blow up the Golden Gate Bridge." And I wouldn't be too anxious to go to the Rose Parade on New Year's Day either! Recently we heard reports that the Statue of Liberty is also in danger!

What is behind these threats? Why have they come upon us suddenly? I believe that the first reason is that God has removed His hand of protection from America because of our national sins – primarily abortion and missing church – and other sins.

But the second root of terrorism also lies in the very nature of mankind. In Deuteronomy thirty-two, we read:

> "For they are a nation void of counsel, neither is there any understanding in them" (Deuteronomy 32:28).

This verse shows that the whole nation was depraved and lost. And the Bible teaches that this was not only true of that nation, but of all nations which reject God. The Bible says, "There is none that understandeth, there is none that seeketh after God" (Romans 3:11). Without the grace of God not a single person would ever be saved.

There is something evil in man's nature that causes him to fight, make war, and terrorize. The Bible says:

> "From whence come wars and fightings among you? come they not hence, even of your lusts that war in your members? [that wage war within you]" (James 4:1).

There is something deep inside the human soul which is evil. Theologians call it "total depravity." Psychiatrists have called it "the id." Philosophers have named it, "the problem of evil." Whatever name it is given – *you have it!* It isn't just the terrorists who are depraved. The Bible teaches that you, too, are depraved, lost in sin, "by nature the children of wrath" (Ephesians 2:3).

You see, the Bible teaches that your very heart is corrupted and hopelessly sinful.

> "Having the understanding darkened, being alienated from the life of God through the ignorance that is in them, because of the blindness of their heart" (Ephesians 4:18).

You often miss church on Sunday. Although this makes you a wicked idolater, you laugh and joke about it. Your very heart is corrupted and opposed to God.

If you become awakened to your sinful condition, you will see how twisted you are inside. You will see how horrible your own heart is. You will see how impossible it is for you to do anything to save yourself in the sight of God.

Only a person who realizes how horribly lost he is has any chance of being saved by Jesus.

> "For the Son of man is come to seek and to save that which was *lost*" (Luke 19:10).

If you do not realize that you are hopelessly *lost*, Jesus Christ, the Son of God, has nothing to offer you.

The Muslim terrorists are attacking us. The source of their fury is Satan and his demons. We have lost the protection of God by turning to sin. For America to survive we must have a mighty revival of true, life-changing Christianity. An old song has these words in it,

> Lord, send a revival, Lord, send a revival,
> Lord, send a revival, And let it begin in me.
>   ("Lord, Send a Revival" by B. B. McKinney, 1886-1952).

Part II

THE BLIGHT OF ISLAM

by

Dr. John S. Waldrip

CHAPTER 6
IS CHRISTIANITY INSUFFICIENT, UNINSPIRED, INADEQUATE, AND IMPOTENT?

Islam is the fastest growing religion in the United States, outpacing even Mormonism in its growth. Los Angeles is the second largest Iranian city in the world behind Tehran,[1] and there are now six million professing Muslims in the United States of America.[2]

The great tragedy of Islam is that it has no answers to the yearnings of the human heart. Islam provides no salvation for anyone's soul. Islam is not the true religion, does not worship the one true and living God, and is at best only a poor counterfeit of Biblical Christianity.

For instance, think of Jesus' instruction toward those who have a different religion. What did Jesus want us to do regarding those who sin against us as individuals? He said they are to be treated as heathens and publicans [tax collectors]. But how did He treat heathens and publicans? He loved them. He ate with them. He befriended them. We should do the same, with courtesy, kindness and respect. That's how we should treat everyone, even those who sin against us.

And what should you do when someone assaults you? In Matthew 5.39 Jesus said, "But I say unto you, That ye resist not evil: but whosoever shall smite thee on thy right cheek, turn to him the other also." When someone assaults you for being a Christian, you are not to resist that evil, but are commanded by Christ to turn the other cheek.

When looking at Islam I urge you to discount the propaganda, I urge you to ignore the lies, and to consider reliable sources. Do you want to know about Islam? Ask any Armenian. Do you want to know about Islam? Ask any Lebanese. Do you want to know about Islam? Ask any Middle Eastern Jew. Do you want to know about Islam? Ask any member of the Bahai or Druse or Greek Orthodox faiths. Ask any missionary to the Middle East. Ask anyone who has dealt with Islam personally.

As for me, I will turn to God's Word as my guide into all truth. And then I will cite sources that serve to illustrate and authenticate what God's Word tells us.

The Founding of Islam Presumes
The Insufficiency of the Bible

How very insulting the whole religion of Islam is to the God of the Bible. After all, the God of the Bible gave to the world the Holy Scriptures, some sixty-six books, written over a 1600-year period of time.

Yet Islam claims that the Bible is not enough, that more is needed, specifically, the Koran. I disagree. I have found the Bible to be more than adequate.

Objectively, the Bible is sufficient because it claims to be. The Bible is the only book that is needed to provide guidance and direction in life, not some other book. Psalm 119:105 declares, "Thy word is a lamp unto my feet, and a light unto my path." And it is God's Word, the Bible, that God uses to prepare us for eternity. As Jesus said to God, in John 17:17, "Sanctify them through thy truth: thy word is truth." And as James put it, "Of his own will begat he us with the word of truth" (James 1:18).

So, what am I to think when I have in my hand a Bible that is completely adequate, without any deficiency, and which pronounces a curse on anyone who would come along afterwards and seek to add written revelation, saying that it is from God? Revelation 22:18-19 says, "For I testify unto every man that heareth the words of the prophecy of this book, If any man shall add unto these things, God shall add unto him the plagues that are written in this book: And if any man shall take away from the words of the book of this prophecy, God shall take away his part out of the book of life, and out of the holy city, and from the things which are written in this book."

So you see, the very concept of Islam rests on the belief that the Bible is insufficient to meet man's spiritual needs.

The Founding of Islam Presumes That The
Christian Bible Was Not Given by Inspiration

God communicated truth to mankind through revelation,[3] truth that could not be discovered by any other means. Inspiration speaks of men writing down that truth for the benefit of later generations.[4]

The two great declarations concerning the revelation and inspiration of the words of the prophets and the apostles are these:

"All scripture is given by inspiration of God, and is profitable for doctrine, for reproof, for correction, for instruction in righteousness: That the man of God may be perfect, throughly furnished unto all good works" (II Timothy 3:16-17).

"For the prophecy came not in old time by the will of man: but holy men of God spake as they were moved by the Holy Ghost" (II Peter 1:21).

These two passages of Scripture tell us that the Bible has been given by inspiration and that the Bible is all we need to instruct and guide us.

But the very existence of Islam denies the inspiration of the Old and New Testaments. Islam denies that the Bible was superintended and overseen by God to exclude any possible error. Islam challenges the truthfulness of God's revelation in the Bible.

You see, the Bible says that God cannot lie. The prophets repeatedly claimed "Thus saith the Lord" and "God said." The apostles wrote such words as "God, who cannot lie" and "Let God be true and every man a liar."

But the very existence of Islam, and the Koran, which is claimed by Muslims to be their Holy Book, is based on the belief that the prophets and the apostles were wrong. *The Koran says that there are mistakes in the Bible. The Koran challenges the inspiration of Scripture.*

By challenging the inspiration of the Old and New Testaments, Islam challenges the truthfulness and honesty of God.

The Founding of Islam Presumes That The Christian Faith is Inadequate

We should remember that the Christian faith came a full five centuries before Islam.[5] That is more than twice the age of the United States. *Islam came along centuries later and told us that the faith presented in the New Testament was not the correct faith. The very existence of Islam supposes that the Christian faith is inadequate and wrong.*

The Founding of Islam Presumes
That The Saviour is Impotent

If Islam did not believe that the Saviour is somehow and in some way impotent, they would not be Muslims, would they? *Instead they would be Christians!*

I have not in any way addressed the specific beliefs of Islam or of any Muslims. I have not downgraded Islam or Muslims in any way. I have not attacked them or suggested hostility toward them. I have only pointed out that the very existence of Islam is based on certain ideas that are contrary to Biblical Christianity.

Since real Christianity is based on a relationship with Jesus Christ, the very existence of Islam supposes something is wrong with the Lord Jesus Christ, or that something is wrong with the Christian conception of Him. Since the Bible teaches that Jesus is the Second Person of the Trinity, and that He is perfect in all His attributes, *Islam's view of Jesus as a mere prophet is an attack on the Christian faith, which is five hundred years older than Islam.*

Please notice that I have not attacked anyone. I have only argued logically and Scripturally from the existence of Islam, and without any substantive comment on the belief system of Islam.

Plainly speaking, Islam is an attack against Christianity. It competes in the marketplace of ideas for the souls of men. If you believe Christianity to be right then you must recognize that Islam is wrong, because the Bible teaches a completely different view of Jesus Christ from that taught by Islam.

But if you believe Islam is right, logically and ethically you should be required to show why a religion 500 years younger is not only superior, but that it is the exclusive vehicle for communicating the will of God to men, and why Christianity not only was wrong for 500 years, but is wrong now.

We are not dealing with Christendom, the sum of all who claim to be Christians, just as we are not now dealing with the Islamic world, containing all those who claim to be Muslims. *We are dealing with real Christianity as it is revealed in the Bible and real Islam as it is presented in the Koran.*

If one is right the other is wrong. If one is right the other is a blight on humanity, because it misguides men and leads them to everlasting destruction. You cannot have it both ways, and you cannot assert that both are "nice religions" – and can't we stop talking about it now? *This issue will not go away, as the events of September 11 have so forcefully proven.*

The origin of Islam is based on certain beliefs. I have restricted myself to the four most groundless beliefs that I could think of: that the Bible is insufficient, that the writings of the prophets and apostles were uninspired, that the Christian faith is inadequate, and that Jesus Christ is unable to save.

Of these four beliefs, it is the last one that strikes at the very heart, and raises the hackles of Biblical Christians. I will not tolerate an attack on the person and work of Jesus Christ, my Lord. I will not sit idly by while any man, or any religion, says that Christ is not able to save us.

Muslims believe Jesus is impotent, that He is only a prophet, and nothing more. But I stand on the sure footing that Jesus is able, not only to save, but to do many other things, with five Scripture verses to support my assertion.

Daniel 4:37

"Now I Nebuchadnezzar praise and extol and honour the King of heaven, all whose works are truth, and his ways judgment: and those that walk in pride he is able to abase."

Jesus is able to abase and humble those who walk in pride. Because He is the King of Heaven, the Sovereign of the Universe, the Creator and Sustainer of this world. Nebuchadnezzar called Him "the King of heaven."

Who said this? Nebuchadnezzar, the man of whom Saddam Hussein, the ruler of Iraq, says he is the reincarnation. If the Lord Jesus Christ can humble Nebuchadnezzar He can surely humble Saddam Hussein!

It was Jesus who humbled Nebuchadnezzar. And it will be Jesus who humbles you, either in this life, to the saving of your soul, or on Judgment Day, before casting you into the lake of fire.

Philippians 3:21

"Who shall change our vile body, that it may be fashioned like unto his glorious body, according to the working whereby he is able even to subdue all things unto himself."

Here the Bible tells us that Jesus Christ can change our vile bodies into glorious bodies, because He is able to subdue all things to Himself.

What person is Jesus unable to subdue? Remember, at the name of Jesus every knee shall bow, and every tongue shall confess that He is Lord.

What power! What might! What regal majesty and omnipotence Jesus Christ, the Son of God, will have in that day!

II Timothy 1:12

> "For the which cause I also suffer these things: nevertheless I am not ashamed: for I know whom I have believed, and am persuaded that he is able to keep that which I have committed unto him against that day."

What was it Paul committed to Christ that he was sure Jesus could keep? It was the safe keeping of his eternal and undying soul. When you are converted, you commit to Jesus Christ the safe keeping of your everlasting soul.

Hebrews 2:18

> "For in that he himself hath suffered being tempted, he is able to succour them that are tempted."

This verse is very hard for a Muslim to swallow. The idea of God becoming a man, the idea of the God-man suffering and being tempted, is repugnant to a Muslim.[6]

But God's ways are higher than our ways and His thoughts are higher than our thoughts. So, you are forced to either believe God or trust human reasoning.

The Bible teaches that Jesus lowered Himself (condescended) to become a man. As a man He was tempted, although He did not sin. And as a man He took upon Himself all of our sins and offered Himself as a sacrifice, the just for the unjust, that He might bring us to God.

Thus, the Son of God is able to offer assistance to us when we are tempted, because He understands temptation from His own earthly experience.

Hebrews 7:25

"Wherefore he is able also to save them to the uttermost that come unto God by him, seeing he ever liveth to make intercession for them."

Here is the pinnacle of the Lord Jesus Christ's ability. He is able to save to the uttermost anyone who comes to God by Him. You need to understand the implications of this verse. *You see, you cannot come to God directly. Jesus said, "No man cometh unto the Father, but by me" (John 14:6). Jesus is the only path to God, the only Saviour of sinful men's souls. That's bad news for a Muslim, and for anyone else who has not come to Christ.*

But here is the good news: any person who comes to God by Jesus, that is, anyone who comes to Him to get to God, is saved by Him forever, "to the uttermost." In other words, Jesus is able to save you all the way to Heaven.

Conclusion

There is nothing wrong with the Lord Jesus Christ. He is a perfectly wonderful and capable Saviour.

Please understand, I hate no Muslim, but I am in profound disagreement with Islam. I am convinced that Islam is a blight, a plague, that does no man any good, and that does great harm to mankind.

If Islam was wrong about nothing else, its view that Jesus is only a prophet, would be reason enough to cast it off forever as a false religion.

If you think Jesus is unable to save your soul, you dishonor Him. If you think Jesus is unable to save your son or daughter, your husband or wife, you dishonor Him.

And in dishonoring Him how are you any different from the Muslims? At the Last Judgment it will really boil down to only one issue – What have you done with Jesus Christ?

If you come to Jesus now, whether you are a Muslim or Infidel, Kafir or professing Christian, He will not cast you out. He will save and cleanse you, and forgive all your sins.

92

FOOTNOTES

[1]"Iranians Feel At Home in the U.S," CNN Interactive web site http://cnn.com/world/9705/23/IranianAmericans/, posted May 23, 1997.

[2]Watchman Expositor web site, http://www.watchman.org/cat95.htm #1, see "Islam."

[3]Norman L. Geisler, Ph.D., *Baker Encyclopedia of Christian Apologetics* (Grand Rapids, Michigan: Baker Book House, 2000, p. 674).

[4]John R. Rice, D.D., Litt.D., *Our God-Breathed Book: The Bible* (Murfreesboro, Tennessee: Sword of the Lord, 1969, pp. 68ff.

[5]John Ankerberg and John Weldon, *The Facts on Islam,* (Eugene, Oregon: Harvest House, 1998), p. 8.

[6]G. J. O. Moshay, *Who Is This Allah?* (United Kingdom: Dorchester House Publications, 1995), pp. 71ff.

CHAPTER 7
A COMPARISON OF
MOHAMMED AND CHRIST

"Beloved, believe not every spirit, but try the spirits whether they are of God: because many false prophets are gone out into the world" (I John 4:1).

The apostle John reminds his readers that "many false prophets are gone out into the world." There are two things this verse tells us to do to be able to discern between a true prophet and a false prophet. First, "believe not every spirit." That is, don't believe every spirit. Christians need to stop being so gullible that they are easy prey for anyone who claims to represent God.

Second, "try the spirits whether they are of God." And that word "try" translates the Greek word for testing ore to determine whether there is gold or silver present. In other words, John is directing his readers to carefully scrutinize those who claim to be prophets of God, to make sure they are genuine. We are told to test the spirits.

Now we will put both the Lord Jesus Christ and the founder of Islam, Mohammed, to the test.[1] *We will place them in a side by side comparison for the purposes of evaluation, so you can decide which of these men is the true prophet of God and which is the impostor.*

Thus, we shall examine the legitimacy of Islam by subjecting its founder to scrutiny, while at the same time examining the legitimacy of Biblical Christianity by subjecting its Founder to similar investigation. Let us weigh seven considerations for the purpose of comparing and contrasting the Lord Jesus Christ with Mohammed.

The Prophecy of Their Comings Contrasted

The prophecies of the coming of Jesus Christ are well documented in the Old Testament, given long before He was born. Here are a few specific prophecies about the Lord Jesus Christ's coming, and the relevant Scripture passages.

Seven hundred years before He was born, the city of His birth was predicted by the prophet Micah, even though it was not the home city of His parents:

> "But thou, Bethlehem Ephratah, though thou be little among the thousands of Judah, yet out of thee shall he come forth unto me that is to be ruler in Israel; whose goings forth have been from of old, from everlasting" (Micah 5:2).

One thousand years before it occurred David predicted the precise form of Christ's death, though it was a method of execution not then known:

> "For dogs have compassed me: the assembly of the wicked have inclosed me: they pierced my hands and my feet" (Psalm 22:16).

His virgin birth was predicted seven hundred years before it occurred:

> "Therefore the Lord himself shall give you a sign; Behold, a virgin shall conceive, and bear a son, and shall call his name Immanuel" (Isaiah 7:14).

More than four hundred years before His birth His forerunner, John the Baptist, was predicted:

> "Behold, I will send my messenger, and he shall prepare the way before me: and the Lord, whom ye seek, shall suddenly come to his temple, even the messenger of the covenant, whom ye delight in: behold, he shall come, saith the Lord of hosts" (Malachi 3:1).

More than five hundred years before His birth the amount of money for which He was betrayed was predicted to be thirty pieces of silver:

> "And the Lord said unto me, Cast it unto the potter: a goodly price that I was prised at of them. And I took the thirty pieces of silver, and cast them to the potter in the house of the Lord" (Zechariah 11:13).

A thousand years in advance of His death it was predicted that men would gamble for His clothes:

> "They part my garments among them, and cast lots upon my vesture" (Psalm 22:18).

A thousand years in advance it was predicted that His legs would not be broken, as the legs of all others who were executed by crucifixion:

> "He keepeth all his bones: not one of them is broken" (Psalm 34:20).

Seven hundred years before His birth, the Old Testament predicted Jesus' death for sinners:

> "He is despised and rejected of men; a man of sorrows, and acquainted with grief: and we hid as it were our faces from him; he was despised, and we esteemed him not. Surely he hath borne our griefs, and carried our sorrows: yet we did esteem him stricken, smitten of God, and afflicted. But he was wounded for our transgressions, he was bruised for our iniquities: the chastisement of our peace was upon him; and with his stripes we are healed. All we like sheep have gone astray; we have turned every one to his own way; and the Lord hath laid on him the iniquity of us all" (Isaiah 53:3-6).

These are only eight of the hundreds of predictions in the Old Testament that were literally fulfilled by the Lord Jesus Christ, prophecies that were given centuries in advance.

Now search for a prediction of Mohammed's coming. You will not find any. Look in the Koran and look elsewhere, but you will find no prophetic announcement of Mohammed's coming. He appeared without any prior notice or any prophecy.

Their Births Contrasted

I've told you that the place of Jesus' birth was predicted to be Bethlehem.

> "But thou, Bethlehem Ephratah, though thou be little among the thousands of Judah, yet out of thee shall he come forth unto me that is to be ruler in Israel; whose goings forth have been from of old, from everlasting" (Micah 5:2).

I've told you that Jesus was born of a virgin.

> "Therefore the Lord himself shall give you a sign; Behold, a virgin shall conceive, and bear a son, and shall call his name Immanuel" (Isaiah 7:14).

I should also point out that Jesus was named before He was born.

> "And she shall bring forth a son, and thou shalt call his name JESUS: for he shall save his people from their sins" (Matthew 1:21).

Now, consider the birth of Mohammed. Except for passing references to the fact that Mohammed was born into a poor family, that his father died before he was born, and his mother passed away before he was six, leaving him to be raised by a grandmother and an uncle, there are no claims made by Muslims regarding the birth of Mohammed.

So, Jesus' birth was prophesied in advance, while Mohammed's was not. The birth of Jesus was miraculous. He was born of a virgin (Isaiah 7:14; Matthew 1:18-25). But Mohammed had both a mother and a father, making his birth, in contrast to the birth of the Lord Jesus Christ, quite ordinary.

Their Lives Contrasted

First, the life of the Lord Jesus Christ. The Bible declares that Jesus lived His life without sin:

> "For we have not an high priest which cannot be touched with the feeling of our infirmities; but was in all points tempted like as we are, *yet without sin*" (Hebrews 4:15).

The Bible records many signs, wonders and miracles performed by the Lord Jesus Christ: feeding five thousand with a few loaves and fishes, walking on the water, raising the dead, giving sight to the blind, healing the crippled, cleansing the lepers, and casting out demons. These miracles performed by Christ are recorded in the four gospels, Matthew, Mark, Luke, and John.

Also, Jesus claimed to be God, claimed to be the exclusive Saviour of sinful men's souls, claimed to forgive sins, and claimed to give men eternal life.

During His lifetime Jesus did not fight with anyone or attack anyone. As a matter of fact, He actually healed one of the men who arrested Him for trial and crucifixion, after the apostle Peter had wounded him with a sword (ref. Luke 22:50-51).

What about Mohammed's life? Authoritative sources, such as Fazlur Rahman, Ph.D., professor of Islamic Thought at the University of Chicago, and Edwin M. Yamauchi, Ph.D., of the Institute For Religious Research, tell us that *the Koran makes no claim that Mohammed ever worked a miracle.*[2]

And Muslims acknowledge that Mohammed committed sins, but they say that he was somehow cleansed of all unworthy thoughts when he was 12 years old, enabling him to intercede on behalf of sinners.

Mohammed's approach to violence was the exact opposite to that of Jesus. Mohammed was active in the pursuit of open warfare against those who opposed him. At one time, according to Muslim scholars, he commanded an army of 10,000. He ordered the killing of many of his opponents.

So, Christ claimed to *be* God, while Mohammed claimed only to *speak* for God. Christ performed miracles while Mohammed did not. Christ refused to resort to violence, while Mohammed was very violent, and killed many who opposed him. They had very different births, and very different lives.

Their Brides Contrasted

The Lord Jesus Christ never married and never was the father of earthly children, but that doesn't mean He has no bride. Just as Israel is spoken of as a wife to Jehovah in the Old Testament, so the Lord Jesus Christ is spoken of as having a bride. John the Baptist referred to the Lord Jesus as the Bride Groom in John 3:29, and Paul reminded the Corinthians that he had espoused them as a chaste virgin to Christ, in II Corinthians 11:2. The Lord Jesus Christ will someday come back and take His bride to Heaven with Him, His bride being made up of all truly born again Christians. The union between Jesus and His bride is a spiritual union, not a physical one.

Mohammed, on the other hand, had many wives.[3] His first wife, Khadija, was a businesswoman who proposed to him, though he was twenty years younger than she was.[4] So long as she lived Mohammed took no other wives.[5] But when his first wife died he married at least ten women and had a number of concubines.[6] *The youngest wife he took was a nine year old girl named A'isha, who actually brought her toys with her when she married him.*

Although none of Mohammed's sons lived to adulthood, he did adopt a son named Zaid. Later he received a special "revelation" authorizing him to marry Zaid's beautiful wife, Zainab.[7] So you can see, with respect to their brides, there are vast differences between the Lord Jesus Christ and Mohammed, the founder of Islam.

Their Deaths Contrasted

Consider the death of the Lord Jesus Christ. Christ did not die in old age. He did not die the death of someone who was sick or ailing. He died an unimaginably brutal death at the hands of Roman soldiers.

The death of the Lord Jesus Christ was predicted as far back as Genesis 3:15, and in great detail in both Isaiah 53 and Zechariah 12:10. By His death and the shedding of His Blood a number of things were accomplished, including:

1. The fulfillment of many prophecies concerning His death.
2. The satisfaction of God's righteous demand that sins be punished.
3. The forgiveness of sins.

What about Mohammed's death? Islamic scholars tell us that in A.D. 632 Mohammed became ill with violent headaches and a fever, possibly from poison.[8] Before he died he exhorted his followers to remain united, proclaimed the duties of married couples, and gave a few other instructions. Mohammed then died and was buried in the house of his wife A'isha, who had nursed him during his last days.[9]

The "prophet's" tomb at Medina is the second most venerated holy place of Islam, after Mecca.

So, the death of the Lord Jesus Christ in the prime of His physical life, at the age of 33, was an event of cosmic proportions, bringing to a climax God's redemptive purpose in the sacrificial death of His Son to pay for the sins of mankind. The death of Mohammed was the death of an old man who got sick and said a few words before he died.

Their Resurrections Contrasted

The resurrection of the Lord Jesus Christ is foundational to Christianity. First of all, Christ's resurrection was predicted 1000 years before it happened. Second, it occurred despite enemy forces placed at His tomb to prevent any such thing from happening. And third, the Lord Jesus Christ showed Himself alive, with many infallible proofs, after His resurrection.

The women saw Him. The apostles saw Him. The men on the road to Emmaus saw Him. Thomas was invited to thrust his fingers into Jesus' crucifixion wounds. Then the risen Christ appeared to Saul of Tarsus on the road to Damascus. As a matter of fact, when Paul wrote his First Corinthian letter, more than 500 eyewitnesses to Christ's resurrection were still alive, and that was more than twenty years later. *So important is the bodily resurrection of Jesus Christ from the dead that the apostle Paul wrote, "If Christ be not risen, then is our preaching vain, and your faith is also vain" (II Corinthians 15:14).*

What do Muslims say about the resurrection of Mohammed? The story of Mohammed's ascension into Heaven is thought by most Muslim scholars to have been modeled after the ascension of Jesus. But Islam tells of Mohammed's ascension into Heaven without any evidence of a resurrection, and without any significance in Mohammed's death. What did Mohammed's death accomplish? Islam does not claim that it accomplished anything.

Christ's death was redemptive, while Mohammed's was not. Christ's death was sacrificial, while Mohammed's was not. Christ's death was predicted, while Mohammed's was not. Christ's death was meaningful, while Mohammed's was not.

Their Legacies Contrasted

First, the legacy of Jesus Christ. How did the early followers of Christ spread the Gospel? They did so by preaching and teaching, and by suffering martyrdom. Christ's followers did not kill people with the sword, but suffered great persecution at the hands of the Romans, the non-Messianic Jews, and others. Christ's legacy is one of forgiveness, of mercy, of grace, of goodness.

But what of the legacy of Mohammed? His followers were warriors. Islam spread across the face of the earth by a different means.[10] Their message was, "Convert or die by the sword." And many people did convert, for fear of execution. What a different legacy was left by Mohammed from that of Christ!

Conclusion

There are different ways of evaluating a religion to determine whether or not it is from God. You can examine the religion's origin, as we have done, and you can examine the religion's founder.

Consider Jesus. Then consider Mohammed. One was foretold in prophecy, while the other was not. One had a miraculous birth and a miracle-filled life, while the other had the blood of his enemies on his hands. One was celibate until the time of His death and resurrection, while the other had many wives, including a nine year old child, and the wife of his adopted son. One's death was redemptive and full of profound meaning and accomplishment, while the other's was just the ordinary death of an old man. One rose from the dead, with many witnesses attesting to His victory over the grave. The other supposedly did the same, only there were no witnesses. Finally, consider their legacies. The followers of Christ spread the Gospel peacefully by preaching. The followers of Mohammed spread their message by fear and persecution. One founded a religion that is legitimate and that truly represents God, while the other plagues mankind even today.

Christianity is real and Islam is fraudulent. Christianity is the direct result of God intervening in the affairs of men to extend mercy and grace and bring salvation. Islam is the direct result of Satan intervening in the affairs of men to deceive and delude them. I urge you to stop your ears from hearing the doctrines of demons that form the basis of all core Islamic belief and practice. Instead, listen to the good news of Jesus Christ, who came to save you from your sins.

God loves you, according to the New Testament. That is the clear declaration of Scripture and the motive that lies back of all God's dealings with mankind. John 3:16 declares,

> "For God so loved the world, that he gave his only begotten Son, that whosoever believeth in him should not perish, but have everlasting life."

To express His love God sent His own Son. How did He send His Son? By the Virgin Birth. Listen to how the Virgin Mary found this out, recorded in Luke 1:35:

> "And the angel answered and said unto her, The Holy Ghost shall come upon thee, and the power of the Highest shall overshadow thee: therefore also that holy thing which shall be born of thee shall be called the Son of God."

But why did God send His Son? Listen to what Joseph was told, recorded in Matthew 1:20-21:

> "Joseph, thou son of David, fear not to take unto thee Mary thy wife: for that which is conceived in her is of the Holy Ghost. And she shall bring forth a son, and thou shalt call his name Jesus: for he shall save his people from their sins."

This was all done so that God might punish His own Son in your place, for your sins. The Bible says, "The soul that sinneth, it shall die" (Ezekiel 18:4). So, because of your sins, you must suffer death, eternal death, unless Someone who is capable of doing so intercedes for you and satisfies God's demand for punishment of sin. That is precisely why Jesus suffered on the Cross. *God punished His own Son instead of you.* As Romans 5:8 declares:

> "But God commendeth his love toward us, in that, while we were yet sinners, Christ died for us."

Listen to how Paul explained it to the Corinthians:

> "Now then we are ambassadors for Christ, as though God did beseech you by us: we pray you in Christ's stead, be ye reconciled to God. For he hath made him to be sin for us, who knew no sin; that we might be made the righteousness of God in him"
> (II Corinthians 5:20-21).

But you must remember that God will punish you if you reject His Son. You see, your sins are all recorded in God's books in Heaven. And unless you are cleansed by the precious Blood of Christ you will someday be judged for those sins:

> "And I saw the dead, small and great, stand before God; and the books were opened: . . . and the dead were judged out of those things which were written in the books, according to their works" (Revelation 20:12).

And what will happen when you are so judged for your sins?

> "And the sea gave up the dead which were in it; and death and hell delivered up the dead which were in them: and they were judged every man according to their works. And death and hell were cast into the lake of fire. This is the second death. And whosoever was not found written in the book of life was cast into the lake of fire" (Revelation 20:13-15).

This is the way you will be punished for your sins, especially for the sin of rejecting Jesus Christ as your personal Saviour.

God will save you through His Son, if you will come to Jesus. You see, God is merciful and gracious. His mercies endure forever. And He "is not willing that any should perish, but that all should come to repentance" (II Peter 3:9). His great desire is for you to be saved, if only you will.

What does God want you to do? "Believe on the Lord Jesus Christ, and thou shalt be saved" (Acts 16:31). Cast yourself upon Jesus Christ and He will forgive your sins and save you.

FOOTNOTES

[1]William J. Saal, *Reaching Muslims for Christ* (Chicago: Moody Press, 1993), p. 29.
[2]*The Spirit of Islam,* web site, http://www.theperilofislam.com/text/q20.html.

[3]Ibid.

[4]Ibid.

[5]Antranig Chalabian, *Armenia After the Coming of Islam* (Southfield, Michigan: Antranig Chalabian, 1999), p. 32.

[6]Ibid.

[7]G. J. O. Moshay, *Who Is This Allah?* (United Kingdom: Dorchester House Publications, 1995), pp. 85-87.

[8]*The Spirit of Islam,* ibid.

[9]*The Spirit of Islam,* ibid.

[10]William J. Saal, ibid., pp. 31-73.

CHAPTER 8
THE GROWTH OF ISLAM

Before dealing with the growth of Islam, I must admit that no religion can be understood very well by studying the lives of those who are members of that religion. You and I both know so-called Christians who are much more effective at driving people away from the Christian faith than they are at attracting men to it. And the same is true of many terrorist Muslims today. Muslim leaders are appearing on radio talk shows, television shows, and in print media saying, "Please do not judge our religion by those terrorists. They do not represent our religion. We are peaceful."

If that is true then no Muslim should object to an examination of their religion's past. Therefore, we now come more fully to a consideration of Mohammed's legacy, as we review the growth of Islam, and its expansion throughout the world, from its birthplace on the Arabian peninsula.

Starting at the beginning, with both Islam and Christianity, let us compare and contrast how those two religions initially spread over the earth. We will look to the early days of both religions to discover the true character of those religions. We'll start back at the beginning and compare Christianity with Islam..

First, Let Us Compare the Growth of Christianity
And Islam During the Lifetime of the Lord
Jesus Christ and the Lifetime of Mohammed

Consider the spread of Christianity before the Crucifixion of Christ. By looking at the historical record, we find that the Lord Jesus Christ gathered large crowds with His teaching, His preaching, His miracle working, His feeding of the multitudes. Drawing a crowd of interested listeners was never a problem for Someone who gave sight to the blind and who raised the dead. But the large crowds thinned out when He taught things they didn't want to hear, leaving Him with only the twelve apostles: "From that time many of his disciples went back, and walked no more with him. Then said Jesus unto the twelve, Will ye also go away?" (John 6:66-67).

The twelve did not forsake Him until the night before His crucifixion, when Judas betrayed Him for 30 pieces of silver and the others ran away in fear. And when you count the number of followers Jesus had shortly before the day of Pentecost, about two months after His resurrection, the number had grown to 120 (ref. Acts 1:15).

How did the number of disciples grow to 120 over a 3½ year period of time? Was any force used? Was there any coercion? Read the Gospels through from beginning to end and you will find Jesus demonstrating meekness and humility, seeking the salvation of lost souls. Jesus said of Himself, "The Son of man is come to seek and to save that which was lost" (Luke 19:10).

Those who followed Him had no promise of wealth or power. Quite the opposite. He once rebuked two apostles who tried to gain higher positions. Paul, who was called to be an apostle after Christ's resurrection, was quite typical in this regard. Christ told him: "I will shew him how great things he must suffer for my name's sake" (Acts 9:16).

Christ was peace loving and did not attack anyone. His followers were instructed to turn the other cheek when they were persecuted. And the good news was spread by preaching and teaching, without threat of violence to anyone. The violence that came was suffered by Jesus' followers without retaliation.

Quite a different account is given of the growth of Islam during Mohammed's lifetime. In seeking to spread his religion, Mohammed ran into difficulty with those in the city of Mecca, who wanted him returned to the city to face criminal trial. Mohammed gathered raiding parties that attacked the caravans traveling to and from Mecca.

Fazlur Rahman, professor of Islamic Thought at the University of Chicago, writes that Mohammed also had his opponents in the city of Medina killed, and ordered the mass execution of all the men in a Jewish clan who had collaborated with his opponents.[1] By the time of his death Mohammed was the most powerful leader in Arabia. But his path to prominence had cost many lives.

The spread of Christianity during the lifetime of Christ and the spread of Islam during the lifetime of Mohammed were very different. Jesus insisted on peace, dying to self, meekness, and turning the other cheek. His religion grew over the space of 3½ years to about 120 men and women. Mohammed, on the other hand, resorted to violence and the deaths of many who opposed him. By the time of his death Islam controlled most of Arabia.

Next, Let Us Compare the Growth of Christianity And Islam During the First 100 Years After the Deaths of their Respective Founders

Have you ever thought about the spread of Christianity during its first 100 years? As far west as Spain and Great Britain, to the continent of Africa, to India in the east, and far into the north, the Christian religion grew like wildfire, beginning with the miraculous outpouring of the Holy Spirit of God, recorded in Acts chapter 2.

It is a common misconception that the Book of Acts describes the growth of Christianity from Jerusalem to Rome. But the Book of Acts is not really an account of the spread of Christianity from Jerusalem to Rome, since there were already Christians in Rome when Paul wrote to them. What the book of Acts does give us is an insight into the conduct of Christian ministry by the two most prominent leaders, the apostles Peter and Paul.

God worked greatly in their lives, and they were empowered to preach the Gospel of Jesus Christ. They almost always met great opposition when converts were made, resulting in both of them being beaten, imprisoned, and eventually martyred.

So effective were the ministries of the Apostles that it was said of them, "These that have turned the world upside down are come hither also" (Acts 17:6). But how did they turn the world upside down? How did they spread the Christian religion? They were men of peace, who were pacifists in the face of persecution, who did not render evil for evil (ref. I Peter 3.9), and who sought no revenge for wrongs done to them (ref. Romans 12.19). Much blood was shed in order to spread the Gospel and advance Christianity. But it was not the Christians who shed the blood. It was those who opposed them who did that. They themselves shed no blood at all.

This cannot be said for the growth of Islam over a comparable period of time. To be sure, the growth of Islam in its first 100 years was about as great as the spread of Christianity in its first 75 years. But the method by which Islam expanded was exactly opposite from the method employed by Christians in spreading their religion.

When the Muslims came out of the Arabian peninsula, 100 years of nonstop warfare and bloodshed followed. It took only 8 years after

107

Mohammed died to capture Persia, Syria and Egypt. Another 70 years was required to reduce all of North Africa to the Islamic faith.

If Charles Martel, the grandfather of Charlemagne, had not stopped the Muslim army's advance from Spain into what is today France, in A.D. 732, you and I would all be speaking Arabic and praying toward Mecca five times a day.[2] But wherever Islam met those who did not share their faith it was always the same. People were converted with the sword. If a non-Muslim said, "Allah is the one true God and Mohammed is his last prophet," he would then be considered a Muslim and allowed to live.

Raping and pillaging and burning were always associated with the advance of Islam during that time. This is the undeniable history of Islam during its first 100 years. No informed person questions these facts. *How dramatically different from Christianity could a religion possibly be in regard to making converts?* Christianity spread in the first several centuries without the use of physical force, without coercion of any kind, relying solely on the preaching of the Gospel. Islam came along 500 years later and took over several nations already exposed to the Gospel, with the threat of bloodshed used to make Muslims out of these people who were conquered by the sword.

The celebrated Christian historian Philip Schaff made this statement:

> What a difference in the means employed and the results reached! Christianity made its conquest [of the Roman Empire] by peaceful missionaries and the power of persuasion, and carried with it the blessings of home, freedom and civilization. Mohammedanism conquered the fairest portions of the earth [between A.D. 622 and 732] by the sword and cursed them by polygamy, slavery, despotism and desolation. The moving power of Christian missions was to love God and man; the moving power of Islam was fanaticism and brute force.[3]

Notice that we have not yet begun to evaluate what Islam actually believes. When looking at its origin, we examined the necessary suppositions involved in the founding of the religion. Then we examined the life of Islam's founder, Mohammed, and some of the things that he did. And we have looked at the initial spread of Islam, and once again have seen the astonishing contrast between Christianity and Islam.

To this point we have examined what I would call the external evidence related to Islam, and have compared it to Christianity. And this examination reveals that Islam and Christianity have virtually *no similarities* beyond the fact that they are religions of one god. Their claim is based on the Koran. Our claim is based on the Bible. I think our investigation of Islam has already yielded enough information from which to make an informed decision, and we aren't finished yet. The evidence is mounting, and it appears to favor of Christianity over Islam.

For the first one hundred years Islam was a religion that grew by violence, by coercion, by warfare, by intimidation. It was literally spread by the use of force.

Christ, on the other hand, never intended that His kingdom should be advanced the way Mohammed spread Islam. When Christ was brought before Pilate, the Roman governor, shortly before His crucifixion, He said: "My kingdom is not of this world: if my kingdom were of this world, then would my servants fight, that I should not be delivered to the Jews: but now is my kingdom not from hence" (John 18:36). Christ made that statement in response to a question the Roman governor had asked Him: "Art thou the King of the Jews?" And He answered the way He did because His kingdom is not now a kingdom of temporal power and influence. During this present age it is a spiritual kingdom.

In His conversation with Nicodemus, Jesus conveyed a similar thought. He said to Nicodemus, "Except a man be born again, he cannot see the kingdom of God" (John 3:3). Like Pilate, Nicodemus could only envision a kingdom built by force, similar to Islam.

To be sure, spiritual conflict is real warfare. But true Christian warfare is not conducted by force of arms, as Paul related to the Corinthians when he said, "For though we walk in the flesh, we do not war after the flesh: For the weapons of our warfare are not carnal" (II Corinthians 10:4), which is to say, not physical. Christians are not supposed to engage in spiritual conflict by means of physical violence.

Listen to Paul describe the manner of a Christian's spiritual warfare:

> "Finally, my brethren, be strong in the Lord, and in the
> power of his might. Put on the whole armour of God, that
> ye may be able to stand against the wiles of the devil. For

109

we wrestle not against flesh and blood, but against principalities, against powers, against the rulers of the darkness of this world, against spiritual wickedness in high places. Wherefore take unto you the whole armour of God, that ye may be able to withstand in the evil day, and having done all, to stand. Stand therefore, having your loins girt about with truth, and having on the breastplate of righteousness; And your feet shod with the preparation of the gospel of peace; Above all, taking the shield of faith, wherewith ye shall be able to quench all the fiery darts of the wicked. And take the helmet of salvation, and the sword of the Spirit, which is the word of God: Praying always with all prayer and supplication in the Spirit, and watching thereunto with all perseverance and supplication for all saints" (Ephesians 6:10-18).

You can see from Paul's statement that the very idea of advancing the Gospel by physical force, by threats and intimidation, by sword point conversion, by holy warfare, or by any other such means, is foreign to the very nature and character of our Saviour and the early church. And as soon as *anyone* seeks to advance Christianity by forceful means it is no longer true Biblical Christianity that is being advanced, but a perverted and twisted counterfeit that I call "Christendom." *The Roman Catholic Church resorted to violence in the Middle Ages, but by that time it did not reflect the teachings of Christ, which characterized the churches in the first five centuries.*

In all fairness to the Catholics, however, we should remember that the Crusades were attempts to take back land that the Muslims had invaded. Historian Earle E. Cairns says of the Muslim invasions:

The strong North African church disappeared, and Egypt and the Holy Land were lost. The Eastern churches were able to do little more than hold back the Muslim hordes from sweeping past Constantinople... Islam stubbornly resisted the efforts of the papacy and Crusaders to regain the Holy Land.[4]

Although we can sympathize with the Crusaders for wanting to retrieve the lands that Muslims had taken from them by the sword, we must not think that the New Testament teaches war as the way to spread Christianity.

How, then, is the true cause of Christ advanced? How is real Christianity spread? How does a person become a Christian? Certainly not by reciting a phrase, such as Islam demands: "Allah is the true god and Mohammed is his last prophet," or anything like that. Oh, no. Such a conversion as that isn't real conversion at all. Saying a few words, even saying a prayer, never made anyone a true Christian. Becoming a Christian is actually a matter of the heart. And you will never become a Christian until you desire to become one in your heart. Therefore, we must think about what the Bible says about the human heart.

First, Your Heart is Bad

If you are unconverted, you are a lost sinner. And your sin condemns you to Hell so long as it is not forgiven. You have the sentence of eternal damnation hanging over your head. And a truly troubling symptom of your sinfulness is the wickedness of your heart (ref. Jeremiah 17:9). Your heart really is deceitful above all things, and desperately wicked. So wicked, in fact, that you are unconcerned about your heart's wickedness unless you become convicted by God. In and of yourself there is absolutely no hope of you ever becoming a Christian, which means your sins will never be forgiven. You will never be reconciled to God. And you will go to Hell when you die unless God convicts you of sin and converts you.

Second, Real Christianity
Is a Matter of Changing the Heart

Real conversion occurs when a person actually becomes a genuine Christian, when he comes to have saving faith in Jesus Christ, God's Son, the one who suffered and died to pay for our sins.

Paul explains very clearly to us in Romans 10:10 that it is with the heart that a man believes unto righteousness. That is, to become a Christian you must do something more than arrive at an intellectual understanding of the Gospel. You must do something more than Arabs do to become Muslims, which is to recite some words. Praying a prayer isn't enough. Real salvation is a matter of changing the heart. And you must believe in Jesus in your heart, or you will remain lost. But how can you believe in Jesus with your heart, since your heart is wicked and deceitful, and is so strongly opposed to the Lord

Jesus Christ? The fact is, you will never become a Christian until you have a strong desire to become one. So, something must happen to your heart to make you want to come to Christ. Otherwise you will never come to Him.

This Means, Thirdly, That Only When God Changes Your Heart Will You Ever Want to Become a Christian

You cannot change your own heart. You are far too stubborn, too blind, too wicked. And no one else can change your heart, except God. Listen to this verse:

> "The king's heart is in the hand of the Lord, as the rivers of water: he turneth it whithersoever he will" (Proverbs 21:1).

Likewise, your heart is in the Lord's hand, to turn this way or that, just as He does with kings. God must turn your heart and change it. Do you see, then, how Christians are not converted with the sword? Neither are they converted by some other manipulative means, such as an emotional story at the end of a sermon, or by a stirring appeal to patriotism. That approach is entirely ineffective in getting sinners saved. Paul described how he made use of God's Word, made use of faith, made use of truth, made use of prayer, made use of Gospel preaching, as he evangelized the lost. He preached to the hearts of sinners until they desired to come to Christ and be saved.

Finally, Your Heart Must Be Won to Christ For You to Become a Christian

Preaching is the main thing God uses to bring about conversion. "For the preaching of the cross is to them that perish foolishness, but unto us which are saved it is the power of God"(I Corinthians 1:18). But what about the message in the preaching? It is the Cross, the message of Christ's crucifixion. But what is contained in a sermon about the Cross of Christ? Two things: the wrath of God and the grace of God. The Cross of Christ shows us that God punishes sin with great severity, even when it is His Son He is punishing. Oh, how that should make your heart fear! As the song "Amazing Grace" puts it, "'Twas grace that taught my heart to fear." Notice, it must be your heart that fears, since all that is truly important in real Christianity has to do with the heart. There are so many who fear in their "heads," but don't get converted. You must fear God's wrath in your heart.

112

Once the Spirit of God has dislodged you from your lethargy by making you fear His wrath, then comes the other side of the Cross of Christ, which is His great love for you.

Oh, what great love Christ has for us! What a great sacrifice He made by taking upon Himself our sins and suffering the wrath of God on our behalf on the Cross!

Are you not moved when you hear that Christ suffered and bled and died in your place? Don't you think the survivors of the World Trade Center in New York will remember for the rest of their lives the firemen who died in those buildings trying to save them? But Jesus did so much more. What great suffering, what great pain, what great horror He experienced, what great punishment He received to pay for your sins! What great wrath the Father poured out upon His only begotten Son! And it was all for you. Does that move you? If that does not win your heart to Jesus, then you won't be won to Him at all.

So you see, Christians are not converted by being afraid of some warrior's sword, like Muslims were so often converted. Neither is a person converted to Christianity as the result of some man coercing him or manipulating him into "going forward," saying a "sinner's prayer," or being baptized. A Christian is converted when God, by the use of preaching, wins a man's heart, first by holy fear, and then by love. And it is when a man *wants* to become a Christian, *wants* to escape the wrath of God because he has godly fear, *wants* to embrace the love of God in Christ, because his heart has been persuaded that Jesus is the Saviour, that he will believe in Christ with all his heart. Let God make you afraid, and not man. Let the love of God move you. Then come to Jesus Christ with all your heart!

FOOTNOTES

[1]Antranig Chalabian, *Armenia After the Coming of Islam* (Southfield, Michigan: Antranig Chalabian, 1999), pp. 34-35.

[2]Encyclopedia Britannica, web site search "Charles Martel," http://www.britannica.com/search?query=CharlesMartel&ct=.

[3]Philip Schaff, *A History of the Christian Church* (Grand Rapids, Michigan: William B. Eerdmans Publishing Co., 1976), volume 4, p. 150.

[4]Earle E. Cairns, Ph.D., *Christianity Through the Centuries* (Grand Rapids, Michigan: Zondervan, 1981), p. 175.

CHAPTER 9
GOD AND ALLAH CONTRASTED

"There is none other God but
one" (I Corinthians 8:4).

Our entire civilization is timidly locked into the straitjacket of multiculturalism, into the mindless trap of political correctness, and into the confused and syrupy blindness of ecumenicalism. Most of the cultural and religious leaders of this country are so confused that they simply will not believe that the terrorists of September 11th could possibly be anything but a terrible aberration, and that Islam could not be an evil religion. If they admitted that Islam was wrong, then people might have to make value judgments. And our cultural leaders don't want anyone making value judgments.

Our President fully realizes that the American people have no interest in using spiritual discernment to see Islam as it really is. His job is to mobilize the resources of the United States to protect and defend us. And we should support him in that endeavor.

But those reading this book ought to understand that this conflict is considerably more complex, and far more important. You see, while the President is involved in a geopolitical crisis and a new kind of military conflict, you and I are simply seeing a renewal of the age-old conflict between Islam and Christendom.

So far our considerations of "The Blight Of Islam" have focused on the externals, what we can learn from Islam's origin, a comparison of Islam's founder with Jesus, and how Islam was advanced in its early years. Each time we turned to our subject we have done so without dealing to any great extent with the doctrines of Islam.

In this chapter, however, we will begin to examine the theology of Islam, what they actually believe. I promise you an honest consideration of Islamic views as they currently exist, as they are taught by contemporary Muslim scholars, and as they are received by the vast majority of Muslims in the world today, despite their denials and attempts at deception.

Here is an illustration of that deception: we are told by Muslims who appear on television, on the radio, and whose writings appear in print, that Islam is a peaceful religion, just like Christianity. We are told that terrorism is only an aberration, and not the true nature of historical, orthodox Islam. We are told that the word "jihad" is misunderstood and that it refers only to a righteous struggle against injustice and oppression, and that calling for "Islamic jihad" doesn't necessary mean killing and bombing and terrorism.[1]

If that is the case, why did Osama bin Labin call for an "Islamic jihad?" If that is true, why have Iranian clerics in the past called for "Islamic jihad?" Why do the current Islamic terrorist groups refer to their activities as "Islamic jihad?" *Surely these people know their own language.* And surely, if they were misusing their own language or distorting the theology of their own religion, their teachers would speak out against them for doing so.

But that doesn't happen. High ranking Muslim scholars do not correct these statements or demand retractions from these men. And why not? Because *Osama bin Laden, and Hezbollah, and al Fatah, and the other terrorist organizations do not represent extremism in Islam. They are right in the middle of the main theological stream of their religion.*[2]

I have access to several experts who have firsthand knowledge of Muslim theology. I will base what I say on the writings of these men. We will consider only three points of Islamic theology, the revelation of the truth, the inspiration of the truth, and the identity of Allah.

The Islamic View of Revelation

Revelation is the communication of otherwise undiscoverable truth. Islam began with the supernatural visions and revelations that Muhammed claimed he received from Allah through the angel Gabriel, beginning in 610 A.D.[3] The authoritative *Cambridge History of Islam* discusses these revelations by noting that,

> Either in the course of the visions or shortly afterwards, Muhammed began to receive 'messages' or 'revelations' from God...He believed he could easily distinguish between his own thinking and these revelations... Muhammed continued to receive the messages at intervals until his death...Islam began as a consequence of supernatural revelations received by Muhammed. Whatever Islam has accomplished historically, what it is today, it results largely from these supernatural revelations received by Muhammed some 1,400 years ago.

How does revelation in Islam compare with revelation in the Christian religion? To this point, there is no obvious difference between what Muslims and what Christians claim regarding the revealed truths that led to their respective religions.

There are many passages in the Bible which record God revealing truth to men. For instance, II Peter 1:21 speaks of God communicating to mankind: "For the prophecy came not in old time by the will of man: but holy men of God spake as they were moved by the Holy Ghost."

It is not disputed by either Islamic or Christian scholars that God does reveal *truth.* The issue really is this: would God reveal *error* to anyone?

Mohammed received some unusual revelations. On two occasions he received "revelations" that corresponded exactly to the selfish wishes of a friend, after that friend had told Mohammed what he wanted.

On another occasion he received a revelation that corresponded exactly to what his young wife, A'isha (the one who was nine years old when he married her) selfishly desired.[4]

And then there are the revelations allowing him alone to marry as many women as he wanted, while all other men could only marry four wives.[5]

So, our objection is not so much with the Islamic notion of how revelation was accomplished, but with its timing, its content, and its purpose.

The Islamic View of Inspiration

Christianity has a clearly stated position concerning inspiration. II Timothy 3:16 says, "All scripture is given by inspiration of God, and is profitable for doctrine, for reproof, for correction, for instruction in righteousness." The Greek word translated by the English phrase "given by inspiration of God" is "θεοπνευστοσ" (theopneustos) and literally means "breathed out by God." Thus, the Bible claims to be a book that was breathed out by God.

Vitally related to inspiration are the words "verbal" and "plenary." That is, the inspiration of the Bible extends to the specific choices of words in Greek and Hebrew. That's what "verbal" means. The Hebrew and Greek words were given by inspiration. Then, the inspiration of Scripture extends to every portion of the Bible, which is what the word "plenary" means. "Plenary verbal inspiration" means that every Hebrew and Greek word of the Bible, from cover to cover, was given by inspiration. These words have now been translated into many languages.

Of course, if the Bible is inspired, then it is a true record and it is without error, since the Biblical God is repeatedly referred to as One Who is truth, and it is stated that He cannot lie. If there are errors in the Bible, factual mistakes, then the whole idea of its inspiration is called into question. Yet the Christian Bible, scrutinized as it has been over the centuries, is acknowledged to be without error by the leading evangelical scholars of today.

The Koran was written some 500 years after the Bible was completed. Therefore, if the Koran was given by inspiration, it should measure up to the high demands of Biblical inspiration. That is, it would be necessary to expect the Koran to be as internally consistent as the Bible is. Further, it would be necessary to expect the Koran to be as factually correct as the Bible is.

But if you expect the Koran to be internally consistent and to be factually correct, you are wrong. It is neither internally consistent nor factually correct.[6]

For example: One chapter of the Koran (called by them a "Sura") had in the days of A'isha some 200 verses. But after the passage of only a few decades that same Sura had only 73 verses. Muslim scholars acknowledge that 127 verses of the original text were lost and have never been found![7]

Here is a second example: the Koran tells us that Mohammed said that lightning and thunder are two angels, just as Gabriel is an angel.[8] Now, you might think that such a belief is just the opinion of a pre-scientific holy man, but *contemporary Islamic scholars in Egypt and Saudi Arabia agree with Mohammed to this day!*[9]

Here is a third example: the Koran teaches that the world is flat.[10] I know that some will say, "But that's what the Bible teaches, too!" Oh, no, it doesn't. Isaiah 40:22 clearly teaches that the earth is round, and Job 26:7 most definitely shows that the earth hangs in space. *But the Koran, in several places, declares the world to be flat, a doctrine which is believed by Islamic scholars to this day!*[11]

But that's not all. The Koran confuses Miriam, the sister of Moses, with Mary, the mother of Jesus![12] They have the same name in Hebrew. But Mohammed thought that Mary, the mother of Jesus, was the sister of Aaron and Moses.[13] That would make Moses and Aaron Christ's uncles! *In fact they lived 1,500 years apart!*

And do you remember the evil Haman, who conspired in the court of the Persian king during the time of Esther to bring about the deaths of all Jews? Those events happened during the Babylonian captivity, after the Persians had conquered Babylon, and are recorded in the Book of Esther in the Bible. But in the Koran this wicked man, Haman, is represented as the prime minister of Pharaoh, *even though he was born a thousand years afterwards!*

Sadly, these glaring errors are recorded in the Koran, and cannot be defended. They are blindly believed by Muslim clerics and scholars. And the Koran is accepted as true and without error by all orthodox Muslims.

The Identity of the Islamic "Allah"

Who is Allah? What is He Like? Is Allah God? Let us investigate the identity of this being named "Allah" by observing what he has done, recorded in the Koran.

First, the case of the beautiful daughter in law. Mohammed fathered no sons who lived to adulthood, so he adopted a son named Zaid.[14] Zaid married a stunningly beautiful woman named Zainab, who was accidentally seen in scanty attire by Mohammed when he was visiting his son's home.[15]

Mohammed was overcome with lust when he saw her beauty. In the Koran we are told that Allah caused Mohammed's heart to desire Zainab. The Koran teaches that it was Allah's will for Zaid to divorce his wife so his adoptive father, Mohammed, could marry her.[16]

Thus, the Allah of the Koran gave Mohammed the lust he had for his daughter in law, and destroyed the marriage of a young couple, so that Mohammed might marry yet another wife. *This is quite different from the response of the God of the Bible when King David took another man's wife.*

Next, the absence of the love of Allah. Allah in the Koran does not love people as does the God of the Bible.[17] In I John 4:8 and 16 we are told "God is love." And John 3:16 is the most famous verse in the New Testament: "For *God so loved the world,* that he gave his only begotten Son, that whosoever believeth in him should not perish, but have everlasting life."

The Koran lists ninety-nine attributes of Allah,[18] but not a single mention of him loving mankind is found anywhere in that book.[19]

Love is a profoundly important word. It speaks of motives and relationships, of meeting needs, and of the inclination of the heart. But Allah does not love, according to the Koran.[20]

A stark contrast exists between Allah and the God of the Bible, Who not only is love, but loves even those who are opposed to Him. He loves us so much that while we were yet sinners Christ died for us, (ref. Romans 5:8).

Third, we should be concerned about the origin of the name "Allah." All Muslims believe that before Mohammed's time the Arabians were an idolatrous people who worshipped many gods.[21] But they refuse to acknowledge the fact that Allah was the chief of the deities they worshipped, the head of a pantheon of 360 gods worshipped in Arabia before Mohammed's time. However, it can be rather easily proved that Allah was the name of one of the false gods they worshipped before Mohammed's time. Here are two proofs:

First, in the Koran itself (Sura 6:109) it can be seen that pre-Islamic Arabs made their strongest oaths in the name of Allah, because they believed him to be the most powerful of their gods.

Second, the fact that Mohammed's own father was named Abdullah, which means "the servant or slave of Allah," shows conclusively that Allah was the chief deity among Arabs before Mohammed introduced Islam.

These proofs don't show who Allah is. But they do show who Allah isn't. *Allah isn't the God of the Bible. He is not the Christian God! He just isn't God at all! Allah is merely an old tribal god of the pre-Islamic Arabs, whom Mohammed elevated to the position of the sole deity of Islam.*

Thus, two things are obvious that they cannot logically be denied. First, the Koran has no legitimate claim to God-given inspiration, because of its many obvious, factual errors.

Second, Allah is not God. Do not let anyone tell you that Islam and Christianity are in any way related. In spite of some obvious copying of the Bible in the Koran, they are religions which have completely different deities.

The last phrase of I Corinthians 8:4 says, "There is none other God but one."

Christianity and Islam both claim to worship one true God, though Islam believes the Christian concept of the Trinity of God is an impossibility. Nevertheless, Christianity claims to worship one God, and Islam claims to worship one God. *But which religion presents the true God?* There are three things I want you to think about on this matter.

It Is Possible to Mistake Who the True God Is

The entire Arabian people were wrong at one time concerning the true God. They freely admit that they were once idolaters, thus admitting that they were all mistaken.

Therefore, the Arabs were once entirely wrong about this vitally important matter. How can we be sure they are not wrong again? For that matter, how can we be sure Christians are not wrong?

After all, Satan is the great deceiver, is he not? And the human heart is capable of great self-deception, is it not? Therefore, I suggest that we submit both Islam and Christianity to the test of determining which religion is wrong about God.

It Is Not Possible for Both Allah and God To Be the One True God

I say this because things that are different are not the same. And Allah and the God of the Bible are not the same.

God is personal and Allah is impersonal.[22] God is interested in establishing communion with mankind, while the Koran nowhere teaches that this is true of Allah.[23]

God communicates truths about Himself in the Bible, while Allah communicates truths about himself through the Koran.

If one were to study the Koran and then study the Bible, he would quickly conclude that they speak of two different beings when they talk about God. *And this is undeniable, since two beings who are different are not the same.*

It Is Possible to Tell Which Is the One True God

Use your own judgment to arrive at a decision that may well have eternal consequences for you.

Which is the one true God, the one who in the Bible loves and is love, or the one about whom no mention of love is made in the Koran?

Which is the one true God, the one who was displeased and who punished the man who by lust destroyed the marriage of another (King David), or the one who not only sanctioned such lust but initiated it and authorized the ruin of a marriage and the destruction of a home?

Which is the one true God, the one whose Bible is both internally consistent and without either scientific or historical errors, or the one whose Koran is both internally inconsistent, and prone to both historical and scientific errors?

Which is the one true God, the one who makes Himself known to His creatures and seeks communion with them (God), or the one whose followers admit that he is both unknown and unknowable (Allah)?

Conclusion

I have said that things which are different are not the same. I have shown that a comparison of the Bible and the Koran leads anyone who is intellectually honest to conclude that *God and Allah are different – therefore they are not the same.*

Two beings who do not have the same attributes cannot be the same God. Also, since they are not the same, only one can be true, while the other must be false.

I maintain that a reasonable consideration of the facts shows God to be God – and Allah not to be God. Since the God of the Bible is the only true and living God, Allah is an impostor, and his religion is false.

If you are considering the Bible's claims about God and the Koran's claims about Allah, I have given you sufficient information with which to know that Jehovah, the God of the Bible, is the true God.

But that knowledge alone is not enough. Knowing that the Bible is true, and the God of the Bible is the real God, is only the beginning. Unless you are inwardly converted to Christ you are still cut off from God, and your sins remain unforgiven. But at least you can now be confident who God is. The next step is to be reconciled to God through Jesus Christ, His only begotten Son.

FOOTNOTES

[1]G. J. O. Moshay, *Who Is this Allah?* (United Kingdom: Dorchester House Publications, 1995), p. 23.

[2]Ibid, p. 35.

[3]William J. Saal, *Reaching Muslims for Christ* (Chicago: Moody Press, 1993), p. 29.

[4]Abd El Schafi, *Behind the Veil: Unmasking Islam*, pp. 212-213.

[5]Ibid, p. 106.

[6]Ibid, pp. 171ff, 233ff.

[7]Ibid, pp. 244-246.

[8]Ibid, pp. 173-177.

[9]Ibid, p. 175.

[10]Ibid, pp. 175-177.

[11]Ibid.

[12]Ibid, pp. 181-182.

[13]Ibid, p. 181.

[14]G. J. O. Moshay, *Who Is This Allah?*, p. 85.

[15]Ibid.

[16]Moshay, pp. 85-87.

[17]John Ankerberg and John Weldon, *The Facts on Islam,* (Eugene, Oregon: Harvest House, 1998), p. 12.

[18]Moshay, p. 13.

[19]Ankerberg and Weldon, p. 12.

[20]William J. Saal, p. 43.

[21]Moshay, p. 134.

[22]Ankerberg and Weldon, p. 13.

[23]Ibid.

CHAPTER 10
ISLAM'S BIZARRE BELIEFS ABOUT WOMEN

As a Bible-believing Christian I am convinced that Jesus was right when He said, "the truth shall make you free" (John 8:32).

I have had some awareness of the errors of Islam for more than 35 years, since I read a book titled, "The Religions Of Man," and became somewhat familiar with the basic beliefs of the Muslim religion.[1]

My disagreement with Islam came about as a result of my own conversion in 1974. From that time on I became profoundly concerned with the truth for truth's sake. You see, truth is not some abstraction, but is based on facts and information, provided by the one true and living God to His creatures for their benefit. Error comes from another source, from Satan. And error is the confusion, and perversion, and twisting, and distortion of the truth. Whereas truth shows the way to set men free from sin and from spiritual slavery, error serves only to further enslave people.

Those who are opposed to a clear distinction between Christianity and Islam are confused about the importance of truth and the horrors of spiritual bondage. They have no real grasp of the issues involved, which are the salvation of sinful souls, the setting at liberty those who are captives, and escaping from damnation. So I make no apologies for the course I have set. Sin-darkened people need the bright light of God's truth, and they need to be led away from the spiritual darkness of Islam. Therefore, we will continue in our study of Islamic theology by taking up three more considerations.

What do the Koran and Muslims Teach About Men and Women?

The Bible clearly teaches two concepts about the relationship of men and women, and their standing before God as Christians.

1. First, God's plan is for a functional hierarchy to exist in the home, with the husband acting as the spiritual leader and the wife acting as his helper. This is taught all through the Bible and is denied

only by feminists who want to alter the clear teachings of the Scriptures. The first ten verses of the eleventh chapter of I Corinthians deal with this subject, as do many other passages in the New Testament.

2. Alongside the functional hierarchy that is found in the Bible regarding the Christian home is the spiritual equality of men and women in the sight of God. *The New Testament declares the absolute spiritual equality in the sight of God of every Christian – both men and women:* "There is neither Jew nor Greek, there is neither bond nor free, there is neither male nor female: for ye are all one in Christ Jesus" (Galatians 3:28).

3. Then, the New Testament speaks of how the Christian man ought to treat his wife: "Likewise, ye husbands, dwell with them according to knowledge, giving honour unto the wife, as unto the weaker vessel, and as being heirs together of the grace of life; that your prayers be not hindered" (I Peter 3:7).

4. A Muslim man expects his wife to accommodate him, while a man who is a true Christian realizes that his responsibility for his wife includes accommodating her, and that such accommodation in no way diminishes his position as the leader in his home.

Now, consider what the Koran teaches (and all contemporary Islamic scholars accept) about the relationship between men and women.

1. In Sura 4:34 husbands are directed to beat (scourge) wives whom they feel are in rebellion against them. And this is not just an old view, but is agreed to by contemporary Muslim scholars, who unanimously teach that if a wife is rebellious she is to be rebuked, then favors are to be withheld from her and given to another woman. Furthermore, she is to be beaten if

necessary, so long as the husband doesn't break any of her bones or shed any of her blood.[2]

2. It is universally held by contemporary Muslim scholars that a father may arrange the marriage of his virgin daughter without her permission. As a matter of fact, the daughter doesn't even have to be consulted by her father or the groom.[3] Sons, however, cannot be married off by their fathers without their permission.[4]

3. Mohammed legalized contract marriage,[5] then made it illegal, and then reversed himself again by making it legal before his death.[6] Contract marriage is observed by Shiite Muslims, who are the dominant sect of Islam in Iran. A man may decide he wants a woman, but only for an evening. So, he arranges a contract with her to be married and then, when the time is up, he divorces her.[7] *How is this different from prostitution?*

4. Women are short on faith and intelligence, according to Islam. That belief was held by Mohammed[8] and by contemporary Muslims. In Islam men and women are not considered equal, as they are in Christianity. And the differences between men and women in Islam are more than functional differences. *Islam teaches that women are intellectually and spiritually inferior.*[9] That is why a woman's testimony counts only one half of a man's testimony in an Islamic court.[10] So, it would take more than two women to offset the opposing testimony of one man in a Muslim court of law.

5. In Islam a man can marry four women, while a woman can marry only one man. A man can divorce a wife by repeating the words "I divorce you" three times, while a woman cannot divorce her husband.[11] And women are put on the same level as a dog or a donkey, since a man's prayers have to be repeated if

a dog, a donkey, or a woman passes in front of him
while he is praying.[12]

What do the Koran and Muslims Teach
About Sins and Punishments?

The Bible teaches that sin is the transgression of God's law. Sin
carries the penalty of death, which can only be repealed by the
punishment of the offender or the punishment of a substitute – Jesus
Christ. But what does the Koran teach about sin? It teaches that
Allah has no plan, burden, or concern to save anyone who is not
already a believer of Islam.[13] Listen to these statements from the
"Ali" translation of the Koran, where "Allah" is translated by our
word "God." Keep in mind that Allah is not the God of the Bible:

1. Sura 3:32. "God [Allah] loveth not those who reject
    Faith."

2. Sura 2:190. God [Allah] loveth not transgressors"
    (This statement is repeated many times in the
    Koran).

3. If Allah does not love sinners, then who does he
    love? Only those who love him (Sura 3:31).

4. Allah loves those who fight wars to spread Islam
    (Sura 61:4).

5. Allah loves the just, the righteous, the kind, those
    who do good, and are neat and clean (Suras 5:14, 45:
    49:9; 60:8; 2:222; 9:108).

6. But what does the Koran say about sin? The Koran
    says you are pure in the sight of Allah when you
    pray, if you wash your face, hands and feet.[14] But
    how does that remove sins?

7. Each chapter in the Koran begins with the statement:
    "In the name of Allah, the most compassionate and
    merciful." But ask a Muslim what Allah has done
    about his sins. He will have no answer.

8. The religion of Islam has no remedy for the sin question.[15] Every child in a Christian church knows the answer to the question, "What can wash away my sins?" ("Nothing but the Blood of Jesus"). But the 1.3 billion people who live in the spiritual darkness of Islam have no answer to that question.

9. What good is a religion that doesn't deal with the problem of sin? Of what possible benefit is any religion that doesn't give a cure for sin?

What Do the Koran and Muslims Teach About End-Time Judgment?

Keep in mind several Christian doctrines that are in contrast with Islam: First, the Bible teaches that none are righteous (ref. Romans 3:11), and that "all have sinned, and come short of the glory of God" (Romans 3:23). The consequence of man's sinfulness is death. "For the wages of sin is death" (Romans 6:23). But the verse goes on to tell us the remedy: "but the gift of God *is* eternal life through Jesus Christ our Lord." The Christian Bible is very clear about the fate of sinners, telling us that all sinners will go to Hell if they are not reconciled to God. Christianity presents Jesus Christ as the remedy for sins. If you believe in Jesus Christ with saving faith, you will not be cast out into Hell, for Jesus said, "Him that cometh to me I will in no wise cast out," (John 6:37).

There is no comparable salvation in Islam. Listen to what one translation of the Koran states about Allah's capriciousness: "Allah misleads whom He will and guides whom He will. He is the All-Mighty, the All-Wise." (Sura 14:4) And in Sura 74:31 we read "Allah leads astray whom He will and guides whom He will." That's very different from what the Bible teaches in II Peter 3.9, "The Lord is...long-suffering to us-ward, not willing that any should perish, but that all should come to repentance."

According to Sura 19:71-72 *all* Muslims will go to Hell. You read that correctly, the Koran indicates that if you are a Muslim you will go to Hell! Of course, the Koran teaches that some Muslims will then be rescued from it. But a true Christian will never go to Hell. The Bible is very clear on this:

> "For God so loved the world, that he gave his only
> begotten Son, that whosoever believeth in him should
> not perish, but have everlasting life. For God sent not
> his Son into the world to condemn the world; but that
> the world through him might be saved. He that
> believeth on him is not condemned..." (John 3:16-18).

Muslims think that once they are in Hell they will be rescued from it.[16] But the Bible teaches that those who go to Hell will never get into Heaven (ref. Matthew 25:46; cf. Revelation 20:14).

In the Bible we are clearly taught that Hell is the punishment for sins, and that sinners go to Hell because of offenses and transgressions against God, and because he has rejected the forgiveness offered by Christ. But Mohammed stated that the majority of the inhabitants of Hell are women,[17] and contemporary Islamic scholars still teach this absurd doctrine.[18]

Why would women be more likely to go to Hell than men? Mohammed said, "It is because of the fact that you curse one another very much and show ungratefulness to your husbands."[19] Are women more prone to curse each other than men? Now, to be sure, it is much easier for women to be ungrateful to their husbands than for men to commit that sin, *since men don't have husbands!* But what kind of madness is it to conclude that more women will go to Hell than men for such reasons as these? If you are confused about sin and Hell and the uncertainty of salvation, then you are in agreement with the Muslims. In Islam there is no certainty of salvation and no guarantee of Heaven.[20] Neither is there anything remotely like a Saviour, such as we have in the Christian faith with Jesus, the Son of God. Even if a Muslim dies in a holy war, there is no guarantee that he will go to heaven.[21] *Mohammed himself said that he was not sure he would go there![22] The founder of Islam didn't know where he would go when he died!*

Compared to Christianity, Islam is a twisted maze of contradictory beliefs, a hodgepodge and a patchwork of "catch-as-catch-can" doctrines, with no coherent theme or message behind them.

On the other hand, the theme of Christianity is grace and salvation. It speaks of God's greatness and goodness, His profound love and provision for man's salvation. But Islam only points to the arbitrariness and aloofness of this being called Allah.

Islam is a religion shot through with injustices and inconsistencies. How else can you explain a man being allowed to beat his wife for some slight reason, while he is allowed to deprive her of affection and go out and arrange a "contract wife" for a few hours of pleasure? And what justice is there for cutting off a starving man's right hand for stealing a boiled egg? Yet that is the pronouncement of Islamic law.[23]

Islam proclaims that women are dirt! What a difference there is between Islam, which counts women as slaves, and Christianity, which counts women as equals in the sight of God!

In I Peter 3:7 we read:

> "Likewise, ye husbands, dwell with them according to knowledge, giving honour unto the wife, as unto the weaker vessel, and *as being heirs together of the grace of life;* that your prayers be not hindered."

Consider with me the implications of this phrase, which literally means "joint-heirs of the grace of life." What can we learn from this phrase in the Bible?

We Can Know that We Have the Grace of Life

This is something that Islam does not offer to a sinner. The concept of grace is never mentioned in the Koran. But this phrase was written by the Apostle Peter (I Peter 3:7) to show that sinners can be saved from their sins, can be saved from the power of sin in their lives, and can someday be saved from the presence of sin – when they go to Heaven.

A Christian husband's behavior toward his wife, a husband's prayer life, and the conduct of the wife, are based upon a relationship with God through Christ.

Also, We Can Know that Men and Women Share God's Grace Equally

There is something wonderfully glorious about a man and a woman, two Christians who are married to each other, who can serve God together, who can grow old together, who can pass through the seasons of life together, who can one day walk the golden shore of Heaven together.

Bible Christianity does not present the same picture as the Koran, which teaches that the woman must walk behind the man, and the woman is the man's slave. On the contrary, the Bible speaks of companionship, of cooperation, of ministry together, for eternity.

Christ bled and died to pay for your sins, so that you might have life. What a pity to marry a woman or a man and not be a joint-heir of the grace of life. You are little better than a Muslim if you are married but not converted. You rob yourself and your spouse of the privilege, of the sheer delight, of the glory, of traveling through life together as God's children.

FOOTNOTES

[1]Huston Smith, *The World's Great Religions* (San Francisco: Harper, 1992).

[2]Abd El Schafi, *Behind the Veil: Unmasking Islam* (Abd El Schafi, 2000), pp. 77-81.

[3]Ibid, pp. 82-83.

[4]Ibid, p. 84.

[5]Ibid.

[6]Ibid, p. 85.

[7]Ibid, pp. 88-91.

[8]Ibid, p. 94.

[9]Ibid, p. 95.

[10]Ibid, pp. 97-98.

[11]Ibid, p. 111.

[12]Ibid, pp. 118-119.

[13]John Ankerberg and John Weldon, *The Facts on Islam,* (Eugene, Oregon: Harvest House, 1998), pp. 17-20.

[14]El Schafi, p. 213.

[15]Ramzi G. Khammar, Middle Eastern missionary, personal observation.

[16]G. J. O. Moshay, *Who Is this Allah?* (United Kingdom: Dorchester House Publications, 1995), p. 96.

[17]El Schafi, p. 92.

[18]Ibid.

[19]Ibid, p. 93.

[20]Ankerberg and Weldom, pp. 23-24.

[21]Ibid, p. 25.

[22]Moshay, p. 96.

[23]El Schafi, p. 293.

CHAPTER 11
ISLAM DENIES CHRIST'S CRUCIFIXION

Ever since the terrorist attack on September 11th, I've been thinking about the Muslims I've known in my lifetime. We once had a couple attending our church for a while. He was a chemical engineer from Louisiana, married to a Muslim woman from Iran. There was Omar, an electrical engineering student at Oregon State University. He couldn't find a job because, as a Palestinian, he didn't qualify for security clearance, which almost every electrical engineer in the United States had to have in those days, no matter what kind of job he applied for.

There is Mike, who owns a computer company and does work on our church computers. And there is Nasrin and her son, Bobby.

There is Yo, who owns an auto repair shop. Yo has a Harley Davidson special police motorcycle, and he has offered on several occasions to let me ride it. Yo was born here in the States, but his parents are from Afghanistan.

Then there was Mohammed, who worked at the Texaco service station nearby. He was also a Muslim, and he loved my little girl. When he read the Old Testament in Arabic he was astonished at how strongly it condemned the wickedness of the Jewish people in Bible times.

And then there is John, who runs a Chevron station near our church. He has given many of our church members free car washes. And when our church ran buses he let us keep an account, so we only had to pay for gas once a month.

I have never known a Muslim whom I didn't like, who wasn't friendly to me. Have you? *So, you must understand that I am not suggesting any action toward Muslim people other than being friendly to them, exhibiting love and concern for them, and seeking to bring them to Christ.* And I say this even though I have a firm conviction that the Islamic religion is completely wrong. Islam is incorrect about the Lord Jesus Christ, and about His saving work on behalf of sinners. That makes the Islamic religion dangerous to the souls of those who believe it.

When you are wrong about the Lord Jesus Christ and about His death, burial and resurrection; when you are wrong about the good news that Jesus saves, you should be answered. So, we will examine what Islam teaches about Jesus, focusing especially on what it teaches about His death, burial and resurrection.

What Does Islam Teach About Jesus?

The Islamic "Jesus" is clearly not the Jesus of the Bible. During Mohammed's lifetime on the Arabian peninsula he was exposed to both Jewish and Christian people, and there are two likely reasons that may well have caused him to misunderstand what orthodox Christians believe about Jesus.[1]

First, it is possible that the elevation of Mary, which was beginning about that time, confused Mohammed, and made him think that Christians believed Jesus to be the product of a physical union between Allah and Mary. But that's a notion as repulsive to Christians as it is to Muslims. More likely is the suggestion that Mohammed picked up some Jewish "slurs" against Christianity. The Koran refers to Jesus as Isa, which seems to be a derivative of Esau, rather than the normal Arabic word for Jesus.[2] And this may well have come about through the use of Jewish humor, which has always been heavy on word play. For instance, "Beelzebub" means "Lord of the dung heap" and is a word play on a god's name that is given in the Gospels. So, it is possible that the non-Messianic Jews of Mohammed' day referred to Jesus as Esau, the profane son of Isaac, to ridicule Christianity.[3]

However it happened, Mohammed ended up thinking that the Christian notion of the Trinity was comprised of the Father, the Son and the Virgin Mary, with the Lord Jesus Christ's title as the Son of God being considered by Mohammed as a clear indication (to him) that Christians believed Jesus to be the product of sexual reproduction between Mary and God.[4] As ridiculous as this sounds to the ears of a Christian, Muslims to this day think this is what Christianity teaches.

Thus, Muslims are completely put off by what they wrongly think we believe about the Lord Jesus Christ, and completely unable to understand the doctrine of the Trinity. The Koran itself teaches that Jesus was miraculously born of a virgin, but it says that only makes Him a unique person, and only a human being; although one who worked many miracles.[5]

Part of their misunderstanding about the virgin birth of Christ is rooted in their belief that mankind as a race is weak, but not inherently sinful.[6] Islam believes that man is basically good, and has no concept of Adam's fall into sin. Thus, if mankind is not inherently depraved, if the human heart is not desperately wicked, then there is no need for a Saviour, is there? And that is what Muslims believe.

But the Jesus of the Bible is profoundly different from the Islamic conception of Him. The human race experienced a catastrophic fall when Adam sinned, a fall of such magnitude, from such a height to such a depth, that mankind is not merely weak. The human race is also evil, depraved, wicked, defiled, and unclean. Islam has no conception of man's sinfulness, which is why Muslims think they can be cleansed and prepared for prayer by washing their faces, hands and feet with water or sand.[7] *There is no realization of mankind's sinful depravity in their belief system.* But it was such a realization that prompted Job to cry out for a daysman, a referee, a go-between, who would lay his hand on both God and man (ref. Job 9:33). Job understood that he had no answer to God as a sinner, and that he needed a mediator. This is exactly the function the Lord Jesus Christ performs (ref. I Timothy 2:5).

I do not have to be able to understand the workings of God to accept them as true when they are spoken of in the Scriptures. Thus, when I am told in the Bible that God became a man, so that He might be both God and man, and as such could reconcile God and man, *I am not being asked to believe that God had sexual intercourse with a woman named Mary!* The Koran twists the Bible by teaching this blasphemy. What I am being asked to believe is that Almighty God is powerful enough to work a great miracle, something unimaginable! He used a virgin as an instrument to fulfill His purpose of preparing a body for His eternal Son to inhabit while on earth. So, Islam's view of Jesus is distorted by an improper view of man, an improper view of sin, an improper view of the Bible, and an improper view of God.

What Does Islam Believe About Christ's Crucifixion, Death, Burial and Resurrection?

You must understand that contemporary Muslims cannot separate in their thinking the Cross on which Jesus died and the crosses which appeared on the flags that the Crusaders carried into battle when they reinvaded the Middle East.

To them the Crusaders were Christian invaders, not armies trying to take back territory that had been seized from them by Muslims several centuries earlier. But the Crusaders understood that they were going to take back land that had been forcefully taken from them by the earlier Muslim invasions. And the Crusader flags invariably had crosses on them. So, the historical "baggage" of the Crusades, coupled with the Koran's lack of clarity on the crucifixion, brings about this confusion in their minds.

In Sura 19:33, Jesus is quoted as saying "So Peace is on me the day I was born, the day that I die, and the day that I shall be raised up to life (again)." So, it seems that the Koran acknowledges that the Lord Jesus Christ died. But the Koran is not internally consistent. Mohammed was so opposed to Jesus being crucified that he actually stated that Jesus did not die on a cross. Sura 4:15 reads "They slew him not nor crucified, but it appeared so unto them." *Muslims believe that the Jews got so confused in their effort to crucify Jesus that they accidentally crucified someone else, thinking it was Him.*[8]

The Koran leads Muslims to disregard anything related to the crucifixion of Christ, because their inadequate view of sin requires no atoning sacrifice. Thus, they are convinced that there was no death for Christ, no burial, and of course, no resurrection. They are convinced that Allah took Jesus directly to Heaven, and that He will someday return to earth, marry, father children, and play a role in the final judgment. Underlying all of these errors concerning the saving work of Jesus Christ is the notion that for Jesus to be arrested, tried, beaten, tortured, unjustly convicted, and then executed by means of crucifixion, *would have been a terrible defeat for Jesus and for God.*

On the other hand, Christians understand that the crucifixion of Jesus, with His subsequent death, burial and resurrection, *was a stupendous victory, and not a defeat at all!* After all, Jesus left Heaven's glory on a mission. And His mission was to redeem lost mankind and satisfy His Father's righteous demand of satisfaction for sins committed against Him. After all, when crimes have been committed criminals have to be punished for their crimes, don't they? Well, Jesus did what He set out to do. He paid the penalty for our sins. He then rose from the dead. *He won the victory!*

Jesus was born of a virgin named Mary, but not by means of human physical reproduction. The New Testament teaches that His birth was a miracle. He lived on the earth, teaching and performing miracles, raising the dead and giving sight to the blind. And then He was arrested, tried, and crucified for crimes He did not commit.

But what was accomplished by Christ's crucifixion, that the Muslims do not see? Salvation! Salvation is a concept foreign to Islam, which can only be demonstrated by God in connection with the crucifixion of His Son, Jesus. For God to save wicked and guilty sinners, His righteousness requires that punishment be meted out for our sins against Him. God could not be holy and just without properly punishing sins. But what if the punishment for sins comes down, not on the sinner, but on Someone else, who is qualified to pay the penalty for sin? *What if Someone steps in to pay the penalty demanded by God for your sins?* When Jesus was born of the virgin Mary, the first step was taken to accomplish that. What Job had agonized for, a "daysman," a person who places one hand on man and the other on God, to reconcile man to God, came to pass. Jesus did that.

The next step occured when Jesus was arrested, tried, and crucified. *This was not a defeat. It was part of God's plan, predicted centuries in advance.* "He hath born our griefs," (Isaiah 53:4). "Wounded for our transgressions,...bruised for our iniquities" (Isaiah 53:5). "The LORD hath laid on him the iniquity of us all" (Isaiah 53:6). These prophecies were written seven centuries before Christ. You see, the Lord Jesus Christ was the substitutionary sacrifice for our sins. I Peter 3.18 summarizes it perfectly, *"For Christ also hath once suffered for sins, the just for the unjust, that he might bring us to God..."*

Islam has no concept of God offering salvation to sinful man. They have a god of power, a god of might, a god to be feared. But their god is not the true and living God. He is not the Father of our Lord Jesus Christ.

God is perfect in all His attributes. God is all powerful. God is all knowing. God is wise. God is good. God is love. But there was no way for God to demonstrate the most sublime of all His attributes, the attributes of His magnificent grace and love, apart from the crucifixion of His Son. That is why Jesus became a man. And that is why He took upon Himself our sins and went to the Cross to pay for them. Then, after dying on the Cross and being buried for three days and three nights, He arose victorious over sin, death, Hell and the grave, because it was not possible for death to hold Him (see Acts 2:24).

The entire theme of the life of Christ is *salvation!* His great sacrifice on the Cross, His glorious resurrection and ascension to His

Father's right hand in Heaven, where He now is – it's all about God providing for the salvation of sinful men. Those who are without a Saviour, who find themselves repulsed by perverse notions and concepts of His incarnation, His crucifixion, His substitutionary atonement, His glorious resurrection and ascension, are not to be hated. ***Rather, they are to be pitied.*** They need to experience the grace and love offered to them by God through the sacrifice of His Son.

> "Jesus saith unto him, I am the way, the truth,
> and the life: no man cometh unto the Father,
> but by me" (John 14:6).

Here is the text of an article from ***Christianity Today,*** which compares Jesus Christ to the other leaders of world religions:

> ***To maintain that each of these leaders is equivalent, however, is to argue not from tolerance but from ignorance.*** Each one had his own distinctive message and mission. And in comparing Jesus with Zoroaster, Buddha, Socrates and Muhammad, we discover a number of unique features in Jesus' life and ministry.
>
> ***First,*** only Jesus came out of a culture which was already monotheistic.
>
> ***Second,*** his death by crucifixion is unique. George Bernard Shaw once remarked rather cynically: "These refined people worship Jesus and take comparatively no account of Socrates and Mahomet, for no discoverable reason except that Jesus was horribly tortured, and Socrates humanely drugged, whilst Mahomet died unsensationally in his bed."
>
> On the other hand, Jean-Jacques Rousseau in "Profession de foi du vicaire Savoyard," *Emile,* wrote: What prejudices, what blindness it takes to compare the son of Sophroniscus with the son of Mary! What distance between the two! Socrates, dying without pain, without disgrace, maintained his character easily to the end.... The death of Socrates, philosophizing quietly with his friends, is the sweetest that one could desire; that of Jesus expiring under tortures, injured, ridiculed, cursed by his entire people, is the most horrible that one might dread.... Indeed, if the life and

death of Socrates are those of a sage, the life and death of Jesus are those of a god.

But Jesus' death on the cross is unique not only in its manner but also in its alleged redemptive meaning. *Neither Zoroaster, Buddha, Socrates nor Muhammad claimed his death would save men from their sins.*

Third, if we exclude later legendary and apologetic accounts, we find that early accounts attribute miracles only to Jesus.

Fourth, only Jesus spoke on his own unquestioned authority. Zoroaster and Muhammad acted as spokesmen for God, while Socrates and Buddha urged every man to consult his own conscience.

Fifth, only Jesus predicted he would be resurrected after his death, and only his followers rest their faith on such an event.

Sixth, only Jesus claimed equality with a sole, supreme deity. According to E. O. James, an authority on comparative religions, "Nowhere else had it ever been claimed that a historical founder of any religion was the one and only supreme deity."

Now one may argue that Jesus was a deceiver, though few have made that charge. Or one may choose to believe with G. Bernard Shaw that Christ was sincere but deluded:

Whether you believe with the evangelists that Christ could have rescued himself by a miracle, or, as a modern Secularist, point out that he could have defended himself effectually, the fact remains that according to all the narratives he did not do so.... The consensus on this point is important, because it proves the absolute sincerity of Jesus's declaration that he was a god. No impostor would have accepted such dreadful consequences without an effort to save himself. No impostor would have been nerved to endure them by the conviction that he would rise from the grave and live again after three days.

C. S. Lewis says Jesus' claim to be equal with deity leaves us only one other choice:

"A man who was merely a man and said the sort of things Jesus said would not be a great moral teacher. He would either be a lunatic — on a level

with the man who says he is a poached egg — or else he would be the Devil of Hell." You must make your choice. Either this man was, and is, the Son of God: or else a madman or something worse. You can shut Him up for a fool, you can spit at Him and kill Him as a demon; or you can fall at His feet and call Him Lord and God. But let us not come with any patronising "nonsense" about His being a great human teacher. He has not left that open to us. He did not intend to.[9]

The Islamic view of Jesus is illogical. They believe that He is neither the Son of God nor a madman. They are wrong. He is no madman. And He is not merely a prophet. He is the Son of God. This is what Jesus said:

> *"I am the way, the truth, and the life: no man cometh unto the Father, but by me" (John 14:6).*

Here are three observations, among the many that could be made, from this rich verse of Scripture.

John 14:6 Tells Us That God is Father to His Children

How bleak is the religion of Islam, that worships a god named Allah, with whom no personal relationship is possible.[10] And is it not the same for you if you are not a true Christian? How are you different from a Muslim? God is not your Father, either. You are not His child. Where, then, can you find comfort for your soul? What fills the emptiness in your heart? Without a Father you are a spiritual orphan, isolated and alone.

Allah has no love for sinners.[11] There is no grace for the needy from Allah. There is no comfort for the afflicted from Allah. Oh, what desolation! What isolation! How meaningless life is without the love of God, without a Heavenly Father!

But my God is the God of all comfort. God, my Father, makes life endurable.

> "Blessed be God, even the Father of our Lord Jesus Christ, the Father of mercies, and the God of all comfort; Who comforteth us in all our tribulation, that

138

we may be able to comfort them which are in any trouble, by the comfort wherewith we ourselves are comforted of God" (II Corinthians 1:3-4).

If you are unconverted, don't you wish you had access to that kind of comfort for your soul? Don't you wish you could be so comforted that you could, in turn, comfort others? The God of the Bible is that kind of Comforter to those who are His children, to those who know Him as their Father. Doesn't your heart long for Him?

John 14:6 Tells Us That There Is a Way to Come to God the Father

Islam denies that Allah is known, or that he is even knowable.[12] But Islamic denials that Allah is knowable have no bearing on knowing the God of the Bible, because Allah is not God and God is not Allah. So, whatever seems to be true to the Muslim about Allah is not true about the Christian God. God's desire to be known by His children is quite different from the aloofness of the "unknowable" Allah.

The Bible is very clear in saying that God seeks communion with humanity. Why did God create Adam in His own image and after His likeness if He did not desire to communicate with him? Why did God give to the children of Israel instructions for the construction of the Tabernacle? He did so for the purpose of dwelling among them (ref. Exodus 25:8).

God's desire has always been to dwell with His creatures, simply because God is good and He blesses us when He lives among us. So, there is a way to dwell with God and for God to dwell with you, in a spiritual sense now, and then more fully and completely in the future. The Bible says:

> "And I heard a great voice out of heaven saying, Behold, the tabernacle of God is with men, and he will dwell with them, and they shall be his people, and God himself shall be with them, and be their God"
> (Revelation 24:3).

For this reality to come to pass, and for God to dwell with His creatures, there must then be a way for us to come to Him.

John 14:6 Tells Us That
Jesus Is That Way

Jesus is the exclusive Saviour of sinners, the unique avenue of approach to God, according to John 14:6. A prophetic description of the Lord Jesus Christ was given in the name "Emmanuel," meaning God with us (Matthew 1:23). Also, Jesus Christ was fully human, yet without sin. Therefore, He and only He is qualified to reconcile sinners to God. Having paid the penalty for our sins with the shedding of His Blood, Jesus, the Lamb of God, takes away the sin of the world. He now sits at His Father's right hand, giving an invitation for sinners to come to Him for forgiveness, for cleansing, for reconciliation to God.

But how can this relationship with God the Father be established? Our God is a consuming fire, and His holy nature prohibits sinful people from approaching Him. God is so holy that directly approaching Him is not possible by anyone as sinful as we are. Therefore a Mediator is required, one who is capable of preparing us and cleansing us before taking us to God. This Mediator is Jesus Christ. By dying on the Cross, and shedding His precious Blood, He prepared the way for us to come to God through Him. If you seek to come to the Father you must come to Jesus. Jesus will cleanse you of all your sins with His Blood. He will establish a relationship between you and the Father. That is why Jesus described Himself as the way to God, and indicated that "no man cometh unto the Father but by me" (John 14:6). That is why His invitation has always been, "Come unto me, all ye that labour and are heavy laden, and I will give you rest" (Matthew 11:28). And that is why His invitation has always been backed with this promise: *"Him that cometh to me I will in no wise cast out"* (John 6:37).

I know that there is an emptiness in your heart. There are times when you can feel it. It's accompanied by a sense of loss and a sense of something missing in your soul. You know that something is dreadfully wrong. Your problem is that you are unconverted. You have no peace with God, no sense of sins forgiven, no comfort for your soul. Islam says this comfort that comes from communion with God is not possible, because they say that Allah doesn't meet human spiritual needs, doesn't forgive sins in this way, doesn't comfort the soul. And Islam is right when it says that about *Allah.* Allah doesn't do any of those things. God, does, however.

Jesus, the eternal Son of the living God, became a man, the God-man. He suffered, bled and died to pay for sin. He rose from the dead literally and physically. He is alive, at the right hand of God in Heaven, saving souls every day. So, I urge you to come to Him, and He will save you, forgive you, cleanse you, impart life to you, and take you to the Father. Then you will know the love of God through Him.

Jesus said:

> "I am the way, the truth, and the life: no man cometh
> unto the Father, but by me" (John 14:6).

FOOTNOTES

[1]G. J. O. Moshay, *Who Is this Allah?* (United Kingdom: Dorchester House Publications, 1995), p. 167.

[2]Ibid, p. 142.

[3]Ibid.

[4]William J. Saal, *Reaching Muslims for Christ* (Chicago: Moody Press, 1993), p. 64.

[5]Ibid, pp. 65, 112.

[6]Ibid, p. 69.

[7]Moshay, pp. 102-103.

[8]Ibid, p. 118.

[9]Edwin M. Yamauchi, "Historical Notes on the Incomparable Christ," *Christianity Today,* October 22, 1971, pp. 7-11.

[10]John Ankerberg and John Weldon, *The Facts on Islam,* (Eugene, Oregon: Harvest House, 1998), p. 12.

[11]Ibid.

[12]Ibid.

CHAPTER 12
NO ALLAH IN HEAVEN

According to the Koran, the "last day" is the time when Allah will judge all men, all spirits, and all animals, according to what they have done.[1] This time is also known as the day of resurrection, and the day of judgment.

Muslims believe that when a man dies his soul enters into a state of unconsciousness until the resurrection occurs, a belief that is somewhat like the Seventh Day Adventist doctrine of "soul sleep."[2] Between the time of the resurrection and the day of judgment Muslims believe that there is an undetermined period of time, that they think will be imposed by Allah for the purpose of stirring up the anxiety and suspicions of unbelievers.[3] During that time period, between the resurrection and the day of judgment, Muslims believe that people will turn to their prophets in the hopes they will intercede for them with Allah.[4] At the judgment, a book of deeds will be opened (Sura 18:50) and each person's good and evil deeds will be weighed on a scale. Those certain to be condemned will be those who have denied Allah's existence and his unity, and those who have ascribed equality with Allah to other gods.[5] Of course, they believe this includes Christians, for asserting that Jesus is equal to God. Although Islam teaches that all Muslims will also go to Hell, they hope their good deeds for Allah will outweigh their evil deeds, and that they will eventually be admitted to paradise.[6] Thus, Muslims believe that they can gain access to paradise even with sins on their record, so long as their good deeds outweigh their bad deeds on Allah's scale.

This may sound superficially like the Last Judgment of the unsaved dead (see Revelation 20:11-15). But consignment to Hell at the Last Judgment does not depend on "bad deeds outweighing good." Those who go to Heaven have had their sins washed away by the Blood of Christ (Revelation 1:5). All whose sins remain on their record are consigned to Hell.

Every religion claims in some way to prepare those who observe it for life after death. If religion did not play at least some role in the preparation of an individual for the life to come, then to what end is the religion practiced? Though this reason for practicing religion is true of every false religion, including Islam, it is not true for those practicing Biblical Christianity. The religion of Biblical Christianity is not practiced primarily for getting one's self ready for the next life, but primarily for getting *others* ready for eternity. Islam, however, just like every other religion in the world, is a religion that is practiced by its adherents for the purpose of preparing themselves for the next life, although it may surprise you how few are the assurances given to a Muslim that he is ready for the next life. We will focus our attention on Islam's view of salvation, and Islam's view of Heaven.

What is the Islamic Theology of How to Be Saved?

Many years ago, shortly after my conversion, I was watching a religious television program that featured an interview with an Islamic teacher. During that interview the Muslim scholar insisted, much to the chagrin of his interviewer, that Islam was a non-redemptive religion. When I shared that with others at different times they wouldn't believe me. But it's true. Muslims are not so much trying to gain salvation when they perform their religion's observances, as trying to ensure that they don't lose what they hope they already have. Contrary to Biblical Christianity, which believes mankind is a depraved and fallen race, Islam believes man's current state is normal and that mankind is not basically sinful. Thus, they believe that such a thing as the new birth is unnecessary. And conversion is not seen by Muslims to be the result of a great miracle. So, the rites and rituals of Islam, the performance of their religious duties, serve to preserve what they hope is theirs already, rather than to gain something they do not have. Let me go over for you the religious duties, sometimes called the "Five Pillars of Islam," that form the common pattern in Muslim society:

First, there is the Muslim confession of faith, the shahada. "There is no god but Allah and Mohammed is Allah's prophet."[7] If this phrase is believed and recited in the hearing of two witnesses the person saying it instantly becomes a Muslim. How very much like contemporary Christian "decisionism" this is, with a "sinner's prayer" making people so-called Christians, whether they've been converted or not. The *shahada* is to be recited every day of a Muslim's life.

Second, there is the ritual prayer, or salat. This takes place five times each day. After the body is prepared through ritual washings with water, or with sand, the person who prays must face Mecca and follow a prescribed plan of gestures while reciting a prayer in Arabic.[8] These prayers can be performed anywhere, but it is expected that men will gather on Fridays to pray in a mosque at midday. Women may also gather at the mosque on Fridays, but they generally pray out of sight of the men. Let me add here, these prayers are not the heart's cry of a supplicant to his god, but the recitation of prescribed prayers from memory in Arabic, though the Muslim may not even understand the words he is speaking if he is a non-Arab.

Third, there are obligatory alms, called zakat.[9] Giving these alms is an obligation that is required of every Muslim according to a rather complex formula that is used to calculate the amount, the method of payment, and who is to receive what is given. Gifts in addition to *zakat* are also permitted.

Fourth, there is the fast of Ramadan, called saum.[10] The Koran requires that during the month of Ramadan, when it is possible to distinguish between a white thread and a black thread (from before sunrise until after sunset), no food, drink, tobacco, or sex is allowed. During the nighttime hours these restraints are not imposed, so Muslims usually stay up late to eat. Sick people, preadolescent children, pregnant women, soldiers fighting a war, and some travelers, are exempt from the Ramadan fast.[11]

Finally, there is the pilgrimage to Mecca, known as the hajj.[12] A trip to Mecca must be made by every Muslim, at least once in a lifetime, if it is physically and financially possible. There are all kinds of rites to be performed along the way. Women are allowed to make the pilgrimage if they are accompanied by a husband or other adult male family member, who acts as a protector. The pilgrimage to Mecca is thought to be a good deed that will be rewarded on the day of judgment.

Islam recognizes that human beings sin, but Islam is based upon the conviction that such sins are not the result of a sinful nature, but of ethical misperceptions.[13] They say that we have the moral power not to sin. We do not need salvation. Rather, men need guidance.[14] And with divine guidance, a man is able to live a life of submission that pleases Allah.

If Islam has any concept of salvation it would be in a collective sense, with a society of people seeking to collectively save themselves by doing good works, so long as they are among true believers (Muslims) and not among those who claim that Jesus is equal to His Father.[15]

One final comment about Islamic salvation. *We could list Jihad (Holy War) as a sixth pillar of Islam.*[16] No matter what public relations representatives say during radio and television interviews, it is the unanimous testimony of all contemporary Islamic scholars that their religion calls for "holy war" whenever and wherever possible, to advance Islam by sword point "conversions." They believe that their religion is for all the world.[17] Thus, to engage in Jihad (holy war) serves to earn extra credit with Allah, so to speak, to ensure that the zealot gets a place in Heaven and stands up well at Judgment Day.

What is the Islamic Theology of Heaven?

Mohammed taught outrageous things about Heaven. The things Mohammed said that Allah told him about Heaven can only be described delicately without offending people. Four observations can be made of what Mohammed said was revealed to him.

First, the wine of paradise.[18] It is quite surprising that a great deal is made in the Koran of the wine that those in paradise will drink. It should be remembered that in two places the Koran forbids the drinking of wine by Muslims. But paradise will be one long party, with "rivers of wine" said to be flowing in three different passages in the Koran. Drinking sprees are utterly forbidden now, but they will be an integral part of life in the hereafter, for faithful Muslims in paradise.

Second, the virgins of paradise.[19] Here is where I have to be very delicate, not dealing with the young boys that the Koran speaks of. In addition to rivers of wine flowing in paradise, the Koran indicates, and contemporary Muslim scholars are in complete agreement, that paradise will be a place where each man will have a palace with 70 mansions in it. In each mansion will be 70 houses. In each house there will be a bed. On each bed are 70 sheets of different colors. And on each sheet is a nymph-like wife, who is perpetually a young virgin. The virgins are always available for the carnal pleasure of the Muslim in paradise. A contemporary Islamic scholar has written that the Koran shows that it is the mission of the believers in paradise to fully satisfy themselves with these women. Is it any wonder that young Muslim men are willing to snuff out their own lives in an act of religious zeal? These Islamic terrorists are seeking to enter a paradise full of willing virgins.

And what a lofty and noble concept of women Islam has! Every faithful Muslim woman granted entrance to paradise will be restored to perpetual youth and virginity so she can be one of the many, many women consigned throughout eternity to fulfill some man's carnal appetites!

Third, the referrals to paradise. Although entrance to paradise is not guaranteed to any faithful Muslim, there is an explanation why the families of terrorists who blow themselves up, or who drive airplanes into buildings, never seem to be unhappy. Did you ever wonder why the mothers and fathers of terrorists always celebrate the deaths of their sons? Though the young Muslim man with a carnal mind and no spiritual discernment looks forward to an eternity in paradise, whooping it up in one long drunken orgy, why are those in his family so excited about his suicide in the name of Islamic jihad? It's because the faithful who go to paradise have the right to intercede for 70 of their relatives.[20] No wonder young Muslim warriors see no need of a mediator between them and God, as Jesus Christ is in Christianity. The terrorists see themselves functioning as "mediators" to Allah on behalf of their loved ones. What debauchery in the name of religion! What blasphemy!

The Koran indicates that all that is required to gain paradise is that you avoid great sins and shameful deeds, only falling into small faults (Sura 53:32). In other words, you can get into paradise if you're not too great a sinner. In paradise, the Muslim looks forward to wine flowing like a river, an innumerable number of willing virgins, as many different kinds of food to gorge himself on as he can imagine, and the right to intercede on behalf of others in his family.

You may wonder how Allah will get anyone's attention to worship him in such a place of debauchery. But you can stop wondering, because in the Muslim paradise Allah is not present. That's right. There is no indication anywhere in the Koran that Allah will be present in paradise.[21] In paradise there will be sensuous enjoyment, but no worship of Allah, no service rendered to Allah, no attention paid to Allah, because *there is no indication that Allah will even be in paradise – if the Koran is a correct guide.*

Anyone who claims that there is a similarity between Islam and Christianity is either completely ignorant, speaking about things he has no knowledge of, or a wicked deceiver.

For the Christian, Heaven is all about communion with God and with Christ, in resurrection glory, cleansed from all sin by the Blood

146

of Jesus Christ. There will be no deviant promiscuity in Heaven. Heaven will be a place of purity and holiness, because God is holy.

Islam is a false religion that is built upon the teachings of a man who had an insatiable sexual appetite, a man who married a nine-year-old girl, a man whose life does not stand up to careful scrutiny as a true prophet of God.[22]

I do not know why more preachers don't speak out against Islam. Perhaps they are afraid that they will be assassinated. I know one Baptist preacher in Washington, D.C. who has a $10,000 price on his head, payable to anyone who kills him. The reason? He wrote and published a tract warning American women not to marry Muslim men. He has a bounty on his head for writing that tract.[23] I am quite sure preachers will justify their "soft line" against Islam with many pious sounding excuses. But the real reason for refusing to sound the trumpet is probably fear, fear of retaliation, fear of reprisal, fear of an unexplained accident. *But where is the fear of God?* We ought to fear God, rather than men!

I might ask you the same question. Where is *your* fear of God? Islam teaches that men are essentially good, therefore salvation is not needed. Men are not evil, they say, only weak and in need of guidance. But that is the opposite of what the Bible teaches, and opposite your own life's experience, if you are honest with yourself. You are not just weak. You know deep in your heart that you are also corrupt, defiled and spiritually dead in trespasses and sins. The wrath of God that is held back from overwhelming you in judgment and condemnation is building in intensity and fury with each passing day.

In the midst of all this, there are four truths that you must not deny, that if you deny you will do so to the damnation of your own soul.

First, you must be saved. Islam maintains salvation is not necessary, but Islam is not correct according to the Bible. By your own lifestyle and refusal of the offer of Jesus Christ to be your Saviour you are saying the same thing. You say it to your children, to your friends, to your coworkers, to everyone else you know. So long as you remain unsaved you are shouting to the world that you think a person does not need to be saved. But let me tell you something, so long as you insist, either by your words or by your actions, that you do not need to be saved, you are calling the God of the Bible a liar.

If there was any other way to rescue you from what you deserve, God would not have sent His Son to suffer and bleed and die to pay for your sins. And the Holy Spirit would not be working to convince you of your need for salvation. Therefore, since the whole Bible shows your need to be saved, since God's wrath is hanging over you, since Jesus suffered and bled and died to save you, and since the Holy Spirit's ministry to the unsaved is to convince you of your need for salvation, you need to stop denying the truth. Stop denying that you need to be saved. You *must* be saved!

But that's not all. You must be saved by <u>Jesus</u>. The Bible says that you can only be saved by Him.

> "Neither is there salvation in any other: for there is none other name under heaven given among men, whereby we must be saved." (Acts 4:12).

You cannot be saved by keeping rules or obeying laws, whether it be the Law of Moses or the Islamic Shariah. The Bible says:

> "For what the law could not do, in that it was weak through the flesh, God sending his own Son in the likeness of sinful flesh, and for sin, condemned sin in the flesh" (Romans 8:3).

In other words, no laws or rules have the power to save sinners. As a matter of fact, *no system of religious deeds can save you.* Isaiah 64:6 declares, "all our righteousnesses are as filthy rags." This applies to any and all religious and ethical systems, including Islam. Jesus, Himself is the only Saviour!

I stated earlier that in every religion people practice it to prepare for the hereafter, except Christianity. Biblical Christianity is practiced by people *already sure of Heaven,* because they have put their faith in Jesus Christ. So, why are we Christians? Not in an attempt to get to Heaven, but because we're already assured of Heaven. And it's a good thing, since the righteous deeds that every religion calls for are judged by God to be filthy rags (Isaiah 64:6). There is only one Saviour. Only one Person is both God and man. Only one Saviour can mediate between God and mankind. And only one Saviour was the substitutionary sacrifice for your sins and for mine. Only one Saviour has conquered sin, death, Hell, and the grave. He is the unique Saviour of sinful souls, and His name is Jesus Christ. You must be saved by Him, or you will burn in Hell. You must be saved by Him, or you will suffer an eternity of torment. You must be saved by Him, or you will feel the force of God's fierce wrath. And Jesus is the *only* Saviour. Who else claimed to be God in the flesh? Who else claimed the authority to forgive sins? Who else took your place on the Cross of Calvary and paid for your sins? You must be saved. But that's not all. You must be saved by *Jesus.*

Why? Because you cannot be saved by anyone other than Jesus. Who could save you but Jesus? No religion can save you, since your righteousnesses are as filthy rags. Islam can't save anyone, because Islam doesn't even believe in salvation in any actual sense. They have no Saviour, no substitute, and no relationship with Allah is even possible, according to the Koran. And you can't save yourself. Saving yourself would require that you deliver yourself from the penalty of your sins. Saving yourself would require that you somehow move yourself to eternal spiritual safety. How are you going to do that? Try delivering yourself from the penalty of striking a police officer. Slap a cop in the face and see how successful you are at escaping the punishment for that sin. Yet you think you can escape judgment for sinning against the Almighty! The fact of the matter is that no one can save you but Jesus. No one has ever claimed to be the Saviour except Him, and no one is able to save people besides Him. So, you must be saved. You must be saved by Jesus. You cannot be saved by anyone other than Jesus.

You must come to Jesus now. Why do I tell you to come to Jesus now? For two reasons:

First, because it is God's will that you be saved, and saved today. Here are two Bible verses which teach that:

> "The Lord is not slack concerning his promise, as some men count slackness; but is longsuffering to us-ward, not willing that any should perish, but that all should come to repentance" (II Peter 3:9).

> "Behold, now is the accepted time; behold, now is the day of salvation" (II Corinthians 6:2).

So, you see, I have Scriptural authority for commanding you to be saved today.

But that's not all. *You must actually come to Jesus.* It isn't enough to simply know the fact that Jesus saves. It's wonderful to know that He saves, but *it's not enough to know that great truth. In addition to knowing that Jesus saves, you must also be united to the Saviour by faith.* And this is where many people fall short of becoming truly converted. They don't actually unite with Jesus by faith.

To put it another way, Jesus told sinners to come to Him. He invites *you* to come to Him. And if you come to Him He will save you from sin and its penalty.

What a grief to God you are in your unconverted state. He loves you beyond human understanding, yet you resist Him and fight against Him. He sent His beloved Son to be your Saviour, yet you reject Him. His Holy Spirit seeks to prepare your heart, yet you grieve Him. Have you ever thought of the lengths to which God has gone to secure your salvation, and what the Saviour endured to pay the price of your salvation from sin and damnation? *How could anyone love you more?* I pray that your hard and cold heart will be melted by God's love for you, by Christ's sacrifice for you, by the Holy Spirit's dealing with you.

Will you think about Jesus for a moment? Will you think of His great love for you, and the great terror that will befall you if you should you continue to reject Him? Now, will you come to this One who loves you so much? Will you give up your struggles to save yourself, give up your struggles in resisting Him, give up your struggles to stand as a lonely and isolated sinner? I urge you to come to Jesus now.

> "Neither is there salvation in any other: for there is none other name under heaven given among men, whereby we must be saved" (Acts 4:12).

FOOTNOTES

[1]William J. Saal, *Reaching Muslims for Christ* (Chicago: Moody Press, 1993), p. 34.

[2]*The Watchman Expositor* web site, profile of Seventh Day Adventism, http://www.watchman.org/profile/sdapro.htm.

[3]Saal, p. 35.

[4]Ibid.

[5]Ibid.

[6]G. J. O. Moshay, *Who Is this Allah?* (United Kingdom: Dorchester House Publications, 1995), p. 83.

[7]*Shahada: the Oath,* http://www.ifgstl.org/html/basics/tawheednf.htm#top.

[8]Saal, p. 36.
[9]Ibid.
[10]Saal, pp. 36-37.
[11]Ibid.
[12]Ibid.
[13]Saal, p. 44.
[14]Ibid.
[15]John Ankerberg and John Weldon, *The Facts on Islam,* (Eugene, Oregon: Harvest House, 1998), pp. 25-26.
[16]Ankerberg and Weldon, p. 11.
[17]Abd El Schafi, *Behind the Veil: Unmasking Islam* (Abd El Schafi, 2000), pp. 56-57.
[18]Moshay, pp. 89-90.
[19]Moshay, p. 84.
[20]El Schafi, p. 280.
[21]Moshay, p. 89.
[22]El Schafi, pp. 83, 212.
[23]Telephone conversation with Rev. Esper Ajaj, pastor of the Arabic Baptist Church, Washington, D.C.

CHAPTER 13
A BLOODTHIRSTY RELIGION

We have been forced to think about Islam by the terrorist attacks of the past few months. Although politicians think it is necessary to deny that terrorism is an essential part of the Islamic religion, the fact is so obvious that only the naïve deny it. Rather than look at the facts concerning Islam, many people choose to believe the statements of the defenders of Islam, who repeatedly claim that Islam is a peace-loving faith and not a violent religion. But can such claims be defended?

Before answering that question, let us consider history. G. J. O. Moshay, in his book, *Who Is This Allah?*, said this:

> As for many Westerners who are bothered about Islamic terrorism in the world today, it is because they are so engrossed with technology that they forgot history. Dr. Jane Smith of Harvard University has clearly shown in a dissertation that even the term "Islam" did not originally mean "submission." Also in *The Spiritual Background of Islam*, Middle East scholar Dr. M. Bravmann reveals that the term "Islam" did not originally mean Mohammed's religion or that of any Jewish patriarchal religion as claimed by Muslims. According to Dr. Bravmann, the word *"Islam" was "a secular concept denoting a sublime virtue in the eyes of the primitive Arab; defiance of death, heroism; to die in battle. The term [Islam] denoted bravery in battle. It did not mean peace or submission.*[1]

Dr. Bravmann shows that Islam did not start out as Muslims claim it did. And Islam is not the religion Muslims claim that it is. It is a religion of "defiance of death, heroism; to die in battle." It did not mean peace or submission!

We can learn a great lesson from the Lord Jesus Christ, given in Matthew 7:15-20:

> "Beware of false prophets, which come to you in sheep's clothing, but inwardly they are ravening wolves. Ye shall know them by their fruits. Do men gather grapes

of thorns, or figs of thistles? Even so every good tree
bringeth forth good fruit; but a corrupt tree bringeth
forth evil fruit. A good tree çannot bring forth evil
fruit, neither can a corrupt tree bring forth good fruit.
Every tree that bringeth not forth good fruit is hewn
down, and cast into the fire. Wherefore by their fruits
ye shall know them."

From this teaching we learn two things: First, there are false prophets
who come in sheep's clothing, who are inwardly ravening wolves.
Second, the way to tell them from true prophets is not by what they
say, but by the fruit they produce. It's by their fruit that you will
know them. Let us now look at the fruit produced by Islam. We will
examine the fruit of Islam as it applies to politics, as it applies to
violence, as it applies to unbelievers, and as it applies to conversions.

First, what Muslims believe about politics. The names of the
predominantly Muslim countries throughout the world include
Afghanistan, Algeria, Azerbaijan, Bahrain, Bangladesh, Brunei,
Burkina Faso, Chad, Comoros Islands, Cyprus, Egypt, Eritrea,
Gambia, Guinea Konakry, Indonesia, Iran, Iraq, Jordan, Kazakhstan,
Kuwait, Kyrgyzstan, Lebanon, Libya, Malawi, Malaysia, Maldives,
Mali, Morocco, Mauritania, Niger, Nigeria, Oman, Pakistan, Qatar,
Saudi Arabia, Senegal, Somalia, Sudan, Syria, Tajikistan, Tunisia,
Turkey, Turkmenistan, United Arab Emirates, Uzbekistan and
Yemen.[2]

Are any of those countries guardians of democracy? *Can you
think of a single one of them that doesn't have a totalitarian state,
ruled over either by a military dictator, a king, or some
revolutionary tribunal?* There may be one, but I can't think of it.
Would you like to guess what kind of religious freedom is enjoyed in
these countries, compared to the kind of religious freedom that is
enjoyed in lands affected by Christianity? The political climate of
those nations influenced by Islam is so oppressive that people want to
get out of Muslim-ruled lands. Would you like to guess whether
these countries' problems are with outsiders clamoring to get in or
with insiders clamoring to get out? *History shows that the spread of
the Christian gospel through Europe and Britain is what gave rise
to the middle class, what gave rise to the whole concept of political
freedoms, and what inspired the great Western democracies that
exist nowhere else in the world, except where they were imposed*

artificially in the aftermath of war, such as happened in Japan, Korea and Taiwan.

The form of government enjoyed in the United States and in the United Kingdom and her Commonwealth countries is a form of government that works only when people are essentially self-governing. Such self-government is nonexistent in Muslim countries, and is rapidly disappearing in Western countries, as Christendom fades into the background. You can rest assured, should a country "go Muslim" and suddenly be taken over by Islam, it will not last long as a democracy, but will slide toward either the secular totalitarianism of Iraq or the religious despotism of countries like Iran or Afghanistan. Here is an example of Islamic politics at work: since 1981 the Bible has been banned in the Malay language, in Malaysia. As well, no religion in Malaysia may even use the words "faith" and "belief" in its literature. How did this come to pass? It occurred when Islam grew to slightly more than 50% of the country's population. That's how Muslims act when they are in charge of things.[3]

Next, what Muslims believe about violence. We know Islam is a bloody and violent religion by reading the Koran. The evidence is there for anyone to examine. We also know that Islam's initial growth from the Arabian Peninsula to the east and west was advanced by war and bloodshed, while the growth of Biblical Christianity was led by peaceful men who lifted no sword to advance the cause of Christ. But Muslims will say, "That was more than a thousand years ago. Today we are a very peaceful people and we abhor violence. It's only the extremists who are violent." Here is an answer, from G. J. O. Moshay:

> In Surah 47:4, Muslims are commanded by Allah to smite the necks of all those who do not accept the teachings of Islam until they are thoroughly subdued, and according to verse 7, they would be helping Allah by so doing.[4]

Now, the obvious question is whether the Koran is believed and practiced today on his point. Rahana Nasir has been my friend for many years. When he converted to Christianity from Islam, he was tortured by his father and uncle before they attempted to drown him. He often said, ***"Yes, Muslims do practice the Koran's teaching about violence today."*** G. J. O. Moshay says:

There are so many incitements against Christians and
non-Muslims running through the pages of the Quran
[Koran] that *we find it hard to believe that anybody
can be a real practicing Muslim now or then and not
hate Christians. It is impossible. Any Muslim who is
not violent (secretly or openly) is hardly a real
Muslim, at least not in the Quranic [Koranic] sense.
It means he has not got the spirit of Islam. A typical
practising Muslim must be violent, especially if he
expects to get any reward in the Muslim heaven.*[5]

Listen to this quotation from a contemporary Islamic book. In the
preface to his book, *The Call of Jihad*, Mallam M. Salih writes,
"What a hypocrite is a man who regards the Jihad [holy war] as an
antiquated duty in Islam."[6]

You can deny the truth about contemporary Islam all you want.
You can pretend that the men who represent Islam at local interfaith
councils are telling you the truth when they say that Islam is a religion
of peace and not violence. *But what do you say to the Armenians
whose family members were slaughtered by the Muslims? What do
you say to the Lebanese whose family members were starved to
death by the Muslims? What do you say to the Nigerians who are
being killed by the Muslims for converting to Christianity?*[7] *And
how about those enslaved and raped by the Sudanese Muslims?*[8] A
young girl, whose picture I hold in my hand as I write this, is named
Saleema. She was gang raped and repeatedly beaten, not in some
remote village, but in the central jail of Pakistan's capital city of
Islamabad. Her crime? She led her Muslim girl friend to Christ.
And what happened to her Muslim friend? The parents executed her
for becoming a Christian. What happened to the parents? Nothing.
They were fully supported by the Muslim government when they
killed her. *This did not happen long ago. It happened within the
last two years!*[9]

Islam is a violent religion. Do you still doubt it? *What about
the Muslim atrocities in East Timor, which our liberal news media
conveniently refuses to cover? Muslim Malaysian soldiers are
killing off Timorese Christians, and burning their churches and
homes, even as I write these words.*[10]

What other religion in the world trains little boys to be suicide
bombers? And don't compare Islam to the Japanese Kamikazes in

World War II. Those Kamikazes were men, and they were in uniform, and they attacked only enemy soldiers. Islam preys upon naïve little children to do their dirty work. Not even the Communists, Nazis, or Kamikazes of World War II stooped to that. In this respect, they are even more insidious in their violence than the Nazis of Hitler's Germany! The religion of Islam is violent, and it cannot be denied. It *was* violent. It *is* violent!

Third, what Muslims believe about non-Muslims. The Bible is very clear that Christians are supposed to love their neighbors as themselves (Matthew 22:39), but there is nothing comparable to that in the Koran. Though he was thought to be a radical in the West, the Ayatollah Khomeini was generally regarded by the followers of Islam as one of the exemplary Muslims of modern times for following in the steps of Mohammed and establishing an Islamic state in Iran.[11] But there were far more innocent people slaughtered in the first few years of his reign than were ever killed under the Shah of Iran, whom he deposed.

Here is what the Ayatollah said about the massacres of non-Muslims in his country: "In Persia *no people* have been killed so far – *only beasts!*"[12] And this was in the 1980s. On another occasion the Ayatollah said, "The purest joy in Islam is to kill and be killed for Allah." He was also quoted as saying, *"In order to achieve the victory of Islam in the world, we need to provoke repeated crises, restore value to the idea of death and martyrdom. If Iran is to vanish, that is not important. The important thing is to engulf the world in crises."*[13] In the Sudan there is an ongoing assault against non-Muslims. Raiding parties kidnap young girls for sale as concubines. The young men are enslaved for manual labor. This is happening right now, even as I write.[14]

Before he fled to Saudi Arabia for refuge, the former Ugandan dictator Idi Amin Dada was responsible for the deaths of more than 100,000 of his countrymen. Why? Because they were not Muslims. When he ruled Uganda, Idi Amin was not considered an "extremist." He was a mainstream Muslim.

If anyone still denies that atrocities are going on in Muslim countries solely because of religion, then remember this: the Taliban supposedly considered turning Osama bin Laden over to an Islamic court. Not a court of law, mind you. Not a U.S. federal court, where he could be tried for crimes against U.S. citizens, but an *Islamic* court. Why an Islamic court? Because non-Muslims are not allowed to testify against a Muslim.[15]

When Muslims speak of equality they are only referring to equality between Muslims. No Muslim can be executed for murdering a non-Muslim, according to Islamic law.[16] But a non-Muslim can be executed for merely swearing at a Muslim.[17] And no non-Muslim place of worship is allowed to be built in a region under Muslim control. Also, places of non-Muslim worship that are damaged or destroyed are not allowed to be repaired or restored under penalty of law in Muslim lands today.[18] No church or synagogue can be built. One that already exists cannot be repaired. And did you know that it is illegal under the Shariah [law] to employ non-Muslims in management jobs? Non-Muslims are not allowed to be elevated to leadership positions,[19] and are not even allowed to tell Muslims what to do.

Finally, and to this all contemporary Islamic scholars agree, if a Christian dresses like a Muslim it is permissible to kill him. If a Christian refuses to give up his seat to a Muslim it is permissible to kill him. And if a Christian is not willing to host a Muslim in his church for three days it is permissible to kill him.

Jesus tells us to love publicans and sinners, while Islam despises such people. Jesus tells us to be good neighbors, while Mohammed urged cruelty and humiliation to all who did not submit to his beliefs. In Christianity the difference between saints and sinners is due to God's saving grace, while Muslims are trained to humiliate all non-Muslims. But someone may say, "The Muslims I know are not this way." The Muslims I know are not like that either. But I don't know Muslims in a Muslim-controlled country, and neither do you, in all likelihood. *Ask the Armenians. Ask the Lebanese. Ask the non-Muslim Arabs in Egypt and Jordan and Israel and Syria and Lybia. Ask the non-Muslims in Malaysia and Indonesia. They will tell you how Islam behaves toward non-Muslims when they control a region.*

Finally, what Muslims believe about conversion. What Muslims believe about conversion depends entirely upon which direction the conversion is taking. *In Muslim countries the penalty for any Muslim converting to another religion is death. If a Muslim becomes a Christian he is executed.*[20] On the other hand, they think it is a wonderful thing for someone to become a Muslim. In certain parts of the world, where Islam is not in control, bounties are paid for conversions. In Tanzania, for instance, money is paid for recruiting a Christian into Islam, and much more is paid if the fellow happens to be a pastor or a priest.[21]

Now, what do these things tell us? They tell us that Islam doesn't believe in conversion as the result of a miracle of God. To the Muslim, conversion is merely turning over a new leaf, changing your mind, and nothing more. This shows how Islam's view of conversion is essentially the same as Christian "decisionism." Decisionism, a term coined in England, is rightly understood by Dr. R. L. Hymers, Jr. and Dr. Christopher Cagan as

> ...the belief that a person is saved by coming forward, raising the hand, saying a prayer, believing a doctrine, making a lordship commitment, or some other external, human act, which is taken as the equivalent to, and proof of, the miracle of inward conversion; it is the belief that a person is saved through the agency of a merely external decision; the belief that performing one of these actions shows that a person is saved.[22]

How very similar is the Islamic view of converting to Islam to the typical approach to evangelism practiced in so many Christian churches these days. To these "decisionists" conversion is merely turning over a new leaf. It is not the *inward* conversion spoken of in the Bible.

Many who are being truly converted to genuine Christianity in Africa and Asia, though they are threatened with martyrdom for their faith, are nevertheless embracing Christ in record numbers. This is because *true conversion changes a person's heart. It is an inward experience.* Hymers and Cagan define conversion as

> ...the result of that work of the Holy Spirit which draws a lost sinner to Jesus Christ for justification and regeneration, and changes the sinner's standing before God from lost to saved, imparting divine life to the depraved soul, thus producing a new direction in the life of the convert. The objective side of salvation is justification. The subjective side of salvation is regeneration. The result is conversion.[23]

What makes a Muslim? A "decision." What makes a true Christian? The inward conversion of a person's heart!

Islam is a non-miraculous religion, utterly dependent upon violence and coercion to expand its influence. For real Christianity to advance, the inner experience of the new birth is absolutely essential.

Muslims do not believe in the miracle of spiritual conversion. The closest they ever get to the Christian concept of conversion is the *shahada*: "There is no god but Allah and Mohammed is his prophet." But how does mouthing a few words alter where a person spends eternity? Saying mere words doesn't change anyone's eternal destiny. That's why so many evangelicals are just as lost after they say the "sinner's prayer" as they were before they said it. Saying words, whether they are Muslim words or Christian words, does not save a person's soul. Jesus said, "Ye must be born again" (John 3:7).

The salvation of a human soul is nothing short of a miracle. Only a real, honest to goodness, sent from Heaven miracle of the new birth can redirect a Hell-bound sinner to Jesus Christ and real salvation.

In the third chapter of John we are told what happens when someone is truly born again:

> "Jesus answered and said unto him, Verily, verily, I say unto thee, *Except a man be born again, he cannot see the kingdom of God.* Nicodemus saith unto him, How can a man be born when he is old? can he enter the second time into his mother's womb, and be born? Jesus answered, Verily, verily, I say unto thee, *Except a man be born of water and of the Spirit, he cannot enter into the kingdom of God.* That which is born of the flesh is flesh; and that which is born of the Spirit is spirit. Marvel not that I said unto thee, *Ye must be born again*" (John 3:3-7).

There were two things that the Lord Jesus Christ said to this Jewish Bible scholar, and they apply to you if you are unconverted.

First, Christ Said That the New Birth Is Necessary

> "Jesus answered and said unto him, Verily, verily, I say unto thee, Except a man be born again, he cannot see the kingdom of God" (John 3:3).

Do you want to see Paradise, Mister Muslim? You need to be born again. Do you want to see Heaven, Mister Gentile? You need to be born again. Do you want to see the Messianic Kingdom, Mister son of Abraham? You need to be born again. If you want to get to Heaven, you need to be born again. The new birth, whatever it is, is not an option. It is absolutely required. Without the new birth you get none of God's blessings. Without the new birth you get only God's wrath. *It is necessary that you be born again.*

Second, Christ Told Us About the Nature of the New Birth

> "Jesus answered, Verily, verily, I say unto thee, Except a man be born of water and of the Spirit, he cannot enter into the kingdom of God. That which is born of the flesh is flesh; and that which is born of the Spirit is spirit" (John 3:5-6).

Experience proves that we can't do right for more than five minutes before we mess things up. We are helpless, not only to *do* right, but also to *think* right. "That which is born of the flesh is flesh." The Christian life can only be lived by those who have experienced a genuine miracle, the miracle of the new birth. And even then there are ups and downs, conflicts and disappointments, spiritual battles that rage, and obstacles to overcome. But if you are born again nothing is the same as it was before.

The main change that happens when a sinner is born again is that his sins are forgiven. Imagine that! All sins forgiven! In God's eyes it's as if the convert had never sinned against Him. But accompanying that forgiveness of sins is also the reception of a new heart. This is astonishing to a sinner who is afraid that he will be disappointing as a Christian. Of course he will be disappointing as a Christian! All Christians are disappointing. But less disappointing than you may think, because when you are born again God gives you a new heart. *You will love what you used to hate and hate what you used to love. Why? Because when you are born again you are given a new heart by God. And where your heart leads you will follow.* But the important factor to consider regarding the forgiveness of sins and receiving a new heart is that it's all done by a miracle of God. It isn't natural. It isn't explainable. It's a miracle. Being a miracle means certain things are taken out of your hands. And you don't need to concern yourself with things God takes care of miraculously.

> "Marvel not that I said unto thee, Ye must be born again" (John 3:7).

FOOTNOTES

[1]G. J. O. Moshay, *Who Is this Allah?* (United Kingdom: Dorchester House Publications, 1995), p. 27.

[2]*The Muslim World* web site, http://chasing.8m.com/.

[3]Moshay, p. 151.

[4]Moshay, p. 22.

[5]Moshay, pp. 25-26.

[6]Quoted in Moshay, p. 35.

[7]*Voice of the Martyrs* web site, http://www.persecution.com/country/index.cfm?action=overview&action =overview&countryid=33.

[8]*Voice of the Martyrs* web site, countryid=41.

[9]*Voice of the Martyrs* web site, "Saleema."

[10]*Voice of the Martyrs* web site, "East Timor."

[11]Moshay, p. 31.

[12]Ibid.

[13]Moshay, p. 32.

[14]*Voice of the Martyrs* web site, countryid=41.

[15]Abd El Schafi, *Behind the Veil: Unmasking Islam* (Abd El Schafi, 2000), p. 127.

[16]El Schafi, p. 128.

[17]El Schafi, p. 144.

[18]El Schafi, pp. 131-133.

[19]El Schafi, p. 138.

[20]El Schafi, pp. 11-19.

[21]Moshay, p. 34.

[22]R. L. Hymers, Jr. and Christopher Cagan, *Today's Apostasy,* Second Edition (Oklahoma City, Oklahoma: Hearthstone Publishing, 2001), p. 17.

[23]Hymers and Cagan, pp. 17-18.

CHAPTER 14
ISLAM HAS NO SOLUTION FOR SIN

"Follow peace with all men, and
holiness, without which no man shall
see the Lord" (Hebrews 12:14).

When you get gasoline from a man named Rashid, or the clerk at a store is named Fatima, or when you drive down a boulevard and see a mosque, then you realize that something is going on that you need to pay attention to.

In 1974 there was one mosque in all of France, but today there are more than 1,600.[1] In Chicago there are more Muslims than there are Methodists.[2] In Los Angeles there are more than 500,000 Muslims. There are now Muslim chaplains in our nation's prisons, in our nation's jail systems, and in our nation's military establishment.[3]

The greatest problem Christendom has when facing the onslaught of the rising tide of Islam is "decisionism." *The weakness and anemia of Christendom in the Western world that results from "decisionism" makes many so-called Christians vulnerable to Islam.* But in China, Malaysia, Nigeria, Indonesia and other countries where there are large Muslim populations, and great persecution of Christians, large numbers of Muslims are coming to Christ. How is this disparity to be explained?

Decisionist Christianity thrives in a safe environment like ours, where there is very little opposition to an empty profession of faith which isn't a true conversion. *But when becoming a Christian is a life and death matter, then there is deep thought, profound reflection, and much soul searching, before a sinner comes to Christ.* The real Christian who counted the cost before coming to Christ is far more likely to serve God no matter what happens. *When a person knows that coming to Christ probably means that he will die, it is far more likely that he will remain faithful when threatened with martyrdom.* That's what I believe explains the growth of vigorous Christianity in other parts of the world. It is not the anemic brand of "decisionist" Christianity we see in the West.

I will now give two "conversion" testimonies of "Christians" who became Muslims. Both of them show the vulnerability of

162

professing Christians who are actually unconverted. Their testimonies were taken from a Muslim web site. The man tells us this:

> I grew up Baptist, in a family of ministers, in rural Mississippi. I attended Morehouse College in Atlanta, so I was exposed to the NOI [Nation of Islam], but I had the good fortune to become friends with an orthodox Muslim who explained to me the difference between NOI and Islam, and the lack of knowledge most NOI have of true Islam. Later, after I left school and began working, I got an internet account, and started to study some of the religions of the world. I had never really been a particularly religious person, due to my somewhat scientific nature [this shows that he never experienced true conversion in his Baptist church]. I always insist on proof. I started to delve deeper into Christianity, and studied it intently on the Web. I was somewhat disdained however by some inconsistencies in the Bible. I principally was troubled by the Trinity, though. I just did not see it...When I read Matthew 19:16-17, and Jesus (peace be upon him) says "Why callest thou me good?", it was clear to me that he was saying that he was not good, and only God was. But most of the Christians seemed to think Jesus was being tongue-in-cheek at this point. I found that I would have to be dishonest to accept this.
>
> Then fortune smiled upon me. I hit a deer with my car. It was out of service for almost a month. During that time, I was unemployed, but had saved money, so I could live (I also have two roommates). I still had my internet account, and I decided to study more. After I had studied the Biblical contradictions, in addition to the inherent idolatry and unscriptural nature of the Trinity, along with other things, I rejected Christianity as a religion. Even Jesus did not seem to teach it, he taught belief in God. I went a time without any religion, thinking maybe it was all a sham. I have a friend who is in the 5% NOI [Nation of Islam], and I saw how much he hated religion, and I decided that I did not want to be like that. I believe that God kept my mind open and my heart from hardening against Him, and I studied Islam. Everything just seemed to fit: a reasoned faith which was very prayerful to keep us on

the straight path, yet did not disdain acquisition of knowledge (the preachers back home loved to rail against education, as if ignorance is preferred by God). Islam seemed to be made for me. A good Muslim was the exact sort of person I aspired to be. After another month of study and prayer, I decided that if Muhammad (peace be upon him) was not a prophet, then there had never been prophets in the first place. The moment of decision came one night when I was reading the Qur'an and I read 21:30, and I read of God expanding his creation. Now, I almost became an astronomer at one point, and I still am interested, and these verses hit me like a sledgehammer. I became fearful of God, and wanted to worship him better.[4]

Then a woman writes:

My first realization about the Christian idea of salvation came after I was baptized into a Southern Baptist church at a young age. I was taught in Sunday School that "if you aren't baptized, then you are going to hell."

My own baptism had taken place because I wanted to please people. My mom had come into my room one evening and I asked her about baptism. She encouraged me to do it. So, the next Sunday, I decided to go to the front of the church. During a hymn at the end of the sermon, I walked forward to meet with the youth minister. He had a smile on his face, greeted me, then sat beside me on a pew. He asked a question, "Why do you want to do this?" I paused, then said, "Because I love Jesus and I know that he loves me." After making the statement, the members of the church came up and hugged me...anticipating the ceremonial immersion in water just a few weeks later [this shows that she never truly experienced conversion to Christ. "Loving Jesus" and being baptized do not bring about true conversion].

During my early years at church, even in the kindergarten class, I remember being a vocal participant in the Sunday School lessons. Later, in my early adolescent years I was a member of the young girls' group that gathered at the church for weekly activities and went on annual retreats to a camp.

During my youth, I attended a camp with older members of the youth group. Though I hadn't spent much time with them before, they recognized me as "the daughter of a youth coordinator" or "the girl who plays piano at special occasions at church." One evening at this camp a man was speaking about his marriage. He told the story about meeting his wife. He had grown up in the US where dating was normal, but in the girl's culture, he could only be with her if they had a guardian with them. Since he liked her, he decided to continue seeing her. Another stipulation is that they could not touch each other until she had been given a promise ring. Once he proposed to her, they were allowed to hold hands. This baffled me, yet held me in awe. It was beautiful to think that such discovery of another person could be saved until a commitment was made. Though I enjoyed the story, I never thought that the same incident could occur again.

A few years later, my parents divorced and the role of religion changed in my life. I had always seen my family through the eyes of a child – they were perfect. My dad was a deacon in the church, well respected, and known by all. My mom was active with youth groups. When my mom left, I took the role of caretaker of my father and two brothers. We continued to go to church, but when visiting my mom on weekends, the visits to churches became more infrequent. When at my dad's home we would gather at night every night to read I Corinthians 13 (which talks about love/charity). My brothers, father, and I repeated this so often that I memorized it. It was a source of support for my dad, though I could not understand why.

In a period of three consecutive years, my older brother, younger brother, and I moved to my mom's house. At that point my mom no longer went to church, so my brothers found church attendance less important. Having moved to my mother's house during my junior year of high school, I was to discover new friends and a different way of life. The first day of school I met a girl who was very friendly. The second day of school, she invited me to her house for the weekend – to meet her family and visit her church. I was automatically "adopted" into her family as a "good kid" and "good influence" for her. Also, I was surprisingly shocked at the congregation that attended her church. Though I was a stranger, all of the women and men greeted me with hugs and kisses and made me feel welcome.

After continually spending time with the family and attending church on the weekends, they started talking to me about particular beliefs in their Church of Christ. This group went by the New Testament (literal interpretation of Paul's writings). They had no musical instruments in church services – only vocal singing; there were no hired preachers, but elders who would bring sermons each Sunday. Women were not allowed to speak in church. Christmas, Easter, and other holidays were not celebrated, wine and unleavened bread were taken as communion every Sunday, and baptism was seen as immediately necessary at the moment that the sinner decided to become a believer. Though I was already considered a Christian, members of this congregation believed that I was going to hell if I didn't get baptized again – in their church, their way. This was the first major blow to my belief system. Had I grown up in a church where everything had been done wrong? Did I really have to be baptized again?

At one point I had a discussion about faith with my mom. I told her about my confusion and just wanted somebody to clear things up for me. I became critical of sermons at all churches because the preachers would just tell stories and not focus on the Bible. I couldn't understand: if the Bible was so important, why was it not read (solely) in the church service?

Though I thought about baptism every Sunday for almost two years, I could not walk forward to be baptized. I would pray to God to push me forward if it were the right thing to do – but it never happened.

The next year I went to college and became detached from all churches as a freshman. Some Sundays I would visit churches with friends – only to feel critical of the sermons. I tried to join the Baptist student association, but felt that things were wrong there, too. I had come to college thinking that I would find something like the Church of Christ but it was not to be found. When I would return home to my mom's house on occassional weekends, I would visit the church to gain the immediate sense of community and welcoming.

In my sophomore year, I spent Sundays singing at the Wake Forest church in the choir because I earned good money. Though I didn't support the church beliefs, I endured the sermons to make money. In October of my sophomore year I met a Muslim who lived in my dorm. He was a friendly guy who always seemed to be pondering questions or carrying a deep thought. One evening I spent the entire evening asking him philosophical questions about beliefs and religion. He talked about his beliefs as a Shia' Ismaili Imami Muslim. Though his thoughts did not fully represent this sect of Islam (since he was also confused and searching for answers), his initial statements made me question my own beliefs: are we born into a religion, therefore making it the right one? Day after day I would meet with him and ask questions – wanting to get on the same level of communication that we had reached at our initial meeting – but he would not longer answer the questions or meet the spiritual needs that I had.

The following summer I worked at a bookstore and grabbed any books that I could find about Islam. I introduced myself to another Muslim on campus and started asking him questions about Islam. Instead of looking to him for answers, I was directed to the Quran. Any time I would have general questions about Islam, he would answer them. I went to the local mosque twice during that year and was happy to feel a sense of community again.

After reading about Islam over the summer, I became more sensitive to statements made about Muslims. While taking an introductory half-semester couse on Islam, I would feel frustrated when the professor would make a comment that was incorrect, but I didn't know how to correct him. Outside of my personal studies and university class, I became an active worker and supporter of our newly rising campus Islam Awareness Organization. As the only female member, I would be identified to others as "the Christian in the group." Every time a Muslim would say that, I would look at him with puzzlement –

because I thought that I was doing all that they had been doing – and that I was a Muslim, too.

I had stopped eating pork and became vegetarian, had never liked alcohol, and had begun fasting for the month of Ramadhan. But, there still was a difference...

At the end of that year (junior year) other changes were made. I decided to start wearing my hair up – concealed from people. Once again, I thought of this as something beautiful and had an idea that only my husband should be able to see my hair. I hadn't even been told about hijab...since many of the sisters at the mosque did not wear it.

That summer I was sitting at school browsing the internet and looking for sites about Islam. I wanted to find e-mail addresses for Muslims, but couldn't find a way. I eventually ventured onto a homepage that was a matrimonial link. I read over some advertisements and tried to find some people within my age range to write to about Islam. I prefaced my initial letters with "I am not seeking marriage – I just want to learn about Islam." Within a few days I had received replies from three Muslims – one from Pakistan/India who was studying in the US, one from India but studying in the UK, and one living in the UAE. Each brother was helpful in unique ways - but I started corresponding with the one from the US the most because we were in the same time zone. I would send questions to him and he would reply with thorough, logical answers. By this point I knew that Islam was right – all people were equal regardless of color, age, sex, race, etc; I had received answers to troublesome questions by going to the Qur'an, I could feel a sense of community with Muslims, and I had a strong, overwhelming need to declare the shahada at a mosque. No longer did I have the "Christian fear" of denouncing the claim of Jesus as God – I believed that there was only one God and there should be no associations with God. One Thursday night in July 1997 I talked with the brother over the phone. I asked more questions and received many more pertinent, logical answers. I decided that the next day I would go to the mosque.

I went to the mosque with the Muslim brother from Wake Forest and his non-Muslim sister, but did not tell him my intentions. I mentioned that I wanted to speak with the imam after the khutbah [religious directed talk]. The imam delivered the khutbah, the Muslims prayed [which includes praising Allah, recitation of the Quran, and a series of movements which includes bowing to Allah], then he came over to talk with me. I asked him what was necessary to become Muslim. He replied that there are basics to understand about Islam, plus the shahada [there is no god but Allah and Muhammad is the messenger of Allah]. I told him that I had learned about Islam for more than a year and was ready to become Muslim. I recited the kalimah...and became Muslim on July 12, 1996, alhumdulillah [all praise due to Allah].

That was the first big step. Many doors opened after that - and have continued to open by the grace of Allah. I first began to learn prayer, then visited another masjid in Winston-Salem, and began wearing hijab two weeks later.

At my summer job, I had problems with wearing hijab. The bosses didn't like it and "let me go" early for the summer. They didn't think that I could "perform" my job of selling bookbags because the clothing would limit me. But, I found the hijab very liberating. I met Muslims as they would walk around the mall...every day I met someone new, alhumdulillah.

As my senior year of college progressed, I took the lead of the Muslim organization on campus because I found that the brothers were not very active. Since I pushed the brothers to do things and constantly reminded them of events, I received the name "mother Kaci."

During the last half of my Senior year, I took elective courses: Islam, Christianity, and Judaism. Each course was good because I was a minority representative in each. Mashallah, it was nice to represent Islam and to tell people the truth about Muslims and Allah.[5]

The the two accounts I have given are the testimonies of young adults who grew up in typical Baptist churches here in the United States. They were not introduced to the essence of Biblical Christianity at all, and neither of them was truly born again before their conversion to Islam. Their testimonies show how easily someone who is not born again, and therefore is still spiritually blind, can become enamored with the false religion of Islam. Because of the rapid growth of Islam in the Western world, there are three undeniable facts facing us.

You Must Make Sure That You Are Converted

Make sure you are one of Christ's own sheep, and not a goat in disguise. The danger is not that you may become a casualty at some point. *If you are not converted you are a casualty already!*

I hear men say, "Pastor, I've examined myself and I think I'm a Christian." That sounds wonderful. But let me tell you something. Jesus said to His disciples, "If any man will come after me, let him deny himself, and take up his cross, and follow me" (Matthew 16:24). What am I to think when I provide some direction to a supposed disciple of Christ and I find him unwilling to deny himself even a little bit?

I hear men say, "Pastor, I've examined myself and I think I'm a Christian." That's wonderful. That's fine. That's a wonderful example of a Christian exercising his priesthood as a believer. But if you are not a *converted* believer, you have no God-given priesthood to exercise! It seems to me that a shepherd is much better at evaluating whether one who is browsing around the flock is actually a sheep or not. Besides, how much practice do you have at discerning between the righteous and the wicked? By what criteria would you distinguish between the saved and the lost? *If I were you I would recognize the extraordinary danger you find yourself in if you are not, in fact, truly converted.*

If you were under arrest you would certainly hire an attorney. But when it comes to the safety of your eternal and undying soul, you seem to be quite content to go on as you are, without seriously examining yourself, to see if you are truly converted. I don't believe your course of action is very wise. *I think you need to ask yourself whether you are indeed converted. I think you need to fasten down a time and a place when you were supposedly converted. I think you need to be able to write out a credible testimony that makes good Scriptural sense. And I think if you can't do that you are probably not converted, meaning not only you but your entire family is at risk in ways you probably don't realize.*

You Should Make Sure Your Spouse is Converted

Do you have any idea how many husbands wonder if their wives are converted? There are many couples each of whom doesn't think the other is truly converted. Let me give you some suggestions for discovering if your spouse is unconverted.

1. No private devotional time? Does your spouse seem to have any personal relationship with God? Or does your spouse just feed off of your relationship with God?

2. No discernment? Does your spouse display an alarming lack of understanding of basic spiritual truths, things so basic that it surprises you that he or she doesn't understand?

3. No humility? Does your wife not have the humility to follow you, but insists on retaining "veto" authority over your attempts to lead her? Or does your husband exhibit absolutely no interest in providing spiritual leadership to you?

If you are married to someone you suspect is lost, you need to confront him or her with your suspicions. A person's reaction to such an expression of concern will tell a lot. *At the very least a genuine Christian will be profoundly grateful for your interest, and will seek pastoral counsel to address the matter.*

Don't go through life with a lost husband or wife. Address the issue. No sensible husband or wife will shut off such an important conversation by saying, "I don't want to talk about it." Excuse me! You live with that person and you don't want to discuss with him or her their eternal destiny? That's absurd!

You Should Make Sure Your Family And Loved Ones Are Converted

How can you make certain that your family and loved ones experience conversion? The same way you would try to get a Muslim converted. So pay very close attention. I am condensing what I have read, what I have gotten from my friend, Dr. Ramzi Khammar (missionary to the Middle East), and a recent acquaintance, Esper Ajaj, who pastors an Arabic speaking Baptist Church in Washington, D. C., and who grew up in Syria.

First, you have to genuinely love the person you want to reach for Christ. Jesus taught us that we should love our neighbor as ourselves. And who is our neighbor? Anyone close enough to you to be involved with you. Love for your neighbor is one of the great distinctions between Christianity and Islam, because Islam only shows interest in people who are Muslims. If you've read as many testimonies of professing Christians who became Muslims as I have, you would also be struck by two things: First, their decisions to become Muslims were not well informed. They were profoundly wrong about the basics of Christianity, usually because of inconsistent and unloving so-called Christians they had known. Also, they felt an emotional need that they thought could be met by Islam. They were wrong, but it is what they felt to be true.

The greatest tragedy is when a person's deceitful heart leads him into the soul-damning religion of Islam. What the child of God has, that no one else has experienced, is the love of God shed abroad in our hearts by the Holy Spirit (ref. Romans 5:5). Do you want to see loved ones and the Muslims come to Christ? Love them with all your heart. That's first in importance.

Second, you have to expose the person to the truth. No matter how long a person has attended Church, if he is not converted he believes some glaring errors about the Christian faith. After all, *something* is keeping him from coming to Christ. Muslims, too, have great misconceptions about Christianity. For instance, they think the Bible is corrupted.[6] They also think that Christianity claims Jesus to be the son of God by means of a physical union between God and Mary, an unspeakable blasphemy that has no basis in the Bible.[7] Third, they think Christians believe in three gods, much like the accusation of Jehovah's Witnesses.[8]

You have to know what the Bible teaches to witness to anyone who is lost, including a Muslim. And you have to know that the Bible is true. Don't be like the woman who once called up a pastor friend and said, "Pastor, what do I believe about this matter?" No, no. Your *own* faith needs to be grounded in the truth of God's Word. And this is so important, since Jesus declared that the truth shall make you free (John 8:32). But it's love that makes men willing to receive the liberating truth of Scripture. So, you must love the lost, and you must be ready to correct error and teach truth to them in a kind and loving way.

Third, you must get that lost person to church. Am I saying that a person who refuses to go to church will not get saved? ***Yes, I am saying that.*** The Christian life is a life that God intends to be lived in the community of the local church.

Christ gave Himself for the church (Ephesians 5:25). Too often decisionists consider only the forgiveness of sins, and ignore the totality of salvation. But the reason Jesus wants people to count the cost when thinking about becoming a Christian (Luke 14:28) is precisely so they will be prepared to do what Christ wants them to do *after* they become a Christian – which necessarily includes a deep commitment to the local church.

Also, it is in church that the most important means of grace occurs, which is Gospel preaching. The Bible says:

> "For the preaching of the cross is to them that perish foolishness; but unto us which are saved it is the power of God...For after that in the wisdom of God the world by wisdom knew not God, it pleased God by the foolishness of preaching to save them that believe" (I Corinthians 1:18, 21).

It is extremely important to get the lost to church! It is a great error for parents not to bring their children to church! *And how wrong-headed is that person who tries to bring a loved one or a Muslim to Christ without bringing that person to church. Where else but in church will they hear strong gospel preaching?*

This passage of Scripture shows that it is extremely important to get lost relatives and lost Muslims into as many church services as possible. Here is what happens when a lost person is hears gospel preaching in church:

> "There come in one that believeth not, or one unlearned, he is convinced of all, he is judged of all: And thus are the secrets of his heart made manifest; and so falling down on his face he will worship God, and report that God is in you of a truth" (I Corinthians 14:24-25).

The Problem of Sin

Islam doesn't believe that you have a sin problem. Islam doesn't believe that the human race has fallen into sin. As a matter of fact, Islam insists that people are only weak and in need of guidance, not sinful and in need of salvation. But do the events of September 11th line up with the Muslim view of man's essential goodness? Were the terrorists merely misguided when they flew those planes into three buildings and murdered more than 3,000 people? Would men who knew the true God murder 3,000 people they believed to be misguided?

Excuse me, but something doesn't add up here. The Muslim view of things doesn't explain the condition of mankind, and it doesn't explain the actions of their terrorist butchers. The reason their view of things doesn't explain what's going on in the world is because the Muslim view is wrong.

Man is not essentially good and only in need of guidance. Man is essentially evil, and with a profoundly serious sin problem. And why is sin such a serious problem? Any amount of sin is serious because sin defiles, sin corrupts, sin dirties, sin contaminates the soul. God's Word says, "Without [holiness] no man shall see the Lord" (Hebrews 12:14).

Dr. Ramzi Khammar was born in Beirut and grew up in the Middle East. He tells me that *Islam's greatest weakness is its complete inability to deal with sin.* He is completely correct in his appraisal. Read the Koran from cover to cover and you will not find anything suggesting how to overcome the issue of man's sin.

Jesus Christ Is The Solution to the Problem of Sin

I know a person is not likely to believe this truth until he is loved in such a way that he wants to accept it. The fact is, people are receptive to things they want to accept. Love is the usual motivation.

So I hope that some Christian you know has loved you with God-given love. I hope your heart has been melted by the love of God in Christ Jesus, with the love of some friend or relative, or through the preaching of God's Word about Christ's love for you.

My desire is that you be treated with such care and affection that you can truly feel the concern God has for your soul, and that you can appreciate the fact that Jesus went to the Cross because He loves you. Unless your heart is opened by God's love, it is not likely that you will accept the truth for what it is, "the power of God unto salvation" (Romans 1:16).

I realize the Muslims don't accept Jesus for who He is, the Eternal Son of the living God, the one who was crucified to pay the ransom price for our sins.[9] But let me ask you a question: *If Jesus isn't the Saviour of sinful souls, then who is?* No one else even claimed to be the Saviour. No one else died on the Cross for the sins of humanity. No one else rose from the dead after three days and three nights, in front of hundreds of witnesses. So, please answer me that one question: if Jesus isn't the Saviour, if He isn't the one who washes away sins with His Blood, if He isn't the one who saves people from their sins, *then who does?* There is salvation from sins in no other person, according to the Bible.

Jesus Christ is the only answer to certain questions, such as the sin question. And sin is a big problem. Sin keeps people out of Heaven. Sin angers God. Sin calls down God's wrath. And Jesus is the only solution to the problem of sin.

"Well, maybe the Muslims are right. I don't think Jesus is who you claim He is," someone may say. My friend, if Jesus is not the Saviour of sinful souls, *then there is no Saviour,* since He is the only man in history about whom that claim is made. So, if Jesus is not the one who saves from sins, then there is no salvation from sins. Are you prepared to deal with that?

How Can Jesus Do You Any Good?

What good does it do you that Jesus died on a Cross, shed His Blood, and rose from the dead 2,000 years ago? *How does that help you?* And how does it help you to know that He suffered and bled and died 2,000 years ago? My friend, these *facts,* important as they certainly are, do you no good whatsoever by themselves. What Jesus did was done 2,000 years ago! What He did was done almost 10,000 miles away! How does some event, no matter how wonderful and marvelous it was, benefit you when it is so far removed in space and time? And even if you were there when Jesus died, or even if you were standing at the opening of the tomb when He rose from the dead, how would that benefit you?

What I am about to tell you is unique to Christianity: God has a way whereby the solution to sin, through the death, burial and resurrection of Christ, *can be applied to your problem.* That's right. There is a means by which you can receive the benefit of what Jesus did long ago and far away, to solve your sin problem. It's faith. That's right, faith. The Bible says, "Therefore being justified by faith, we have peace with God" (Romans 5:1).

Although Mohammed is now dead and buried, Jesus is alive again, risen physically from the dead! After He arose from death He ascended to Heaven, where He now sits at His Father's right hand, ready to save sinners – ready to save you! If you will believe in Him fully, He will save you from your sins. Do you grasp the concept? *It isn't what Jesus did that saves anyone. It is Jesus, Himself, who saves sinners.* That's why Jesus told us, "Come unto me" (Matthew 11:28). That's why the Apostle Paul told the Philippian jailor, "Believe on the Lord Jesus Christ, and thou shalt be saved" (Acts 16:31). That's why you need to come to Jesus, and believe on Him as well.

Overview

To review: My friend, you have a terrible problem. It's sin. And it corrupts and defiles you, and will damn your soul. God hates sin. And since God is holy, He won't allow any amount of sin to come into Heaven. Sin is a terrible problem because the only place for sinners to go for eternity is Hell.

Jesus is the solution to the problem of your sin. *And He'd better be the solution to the sin problem, since there is no other solution.* No one else has ever claimed to solve the sin problem, as Jesus did. So, it's Jesus or Hell. There are no other options.

Think about this. Weigh it with the deliberation it deserves. And then act. For unless you come to Jesus Christ there is no salvation for you. Unless you believe on Him, there is no hope. Many men have died and gone to Hell knowing Jesus to be the Saviour, without having actually come to Him – more people than you can ever imagine. Please don't be one of them. Realize that you will never be saved from your sins unless you come directly to Jesus, for there is no other Saviour. And there is no other faith besides Bible Christianity which even promises to answer the sin problem. If you are not a Christian, not really born again, go to a Bible-believing pastor, listen to his gospel sermons, and speak privately with him about the salvation of your soul. I pray that you will do this soon!

FOOTNOTES

[1]John Ankerberg and John Weldon, *The Facts on Islam,* (Eugene, Oregon: Harvest House, 1998), p. 7.

[2]Ibid.

[3]*Los Angeles Times* web site, http://www.latimes.com, "Muslim Chaplains Play a New Role," October 2, 2001.

[4]Testimony of conversion to Islam, http://www.islamzine.com/ideologies/sects/noi/noi4.html.

[5]*Islam Online* web site, "My Journey to Islam," by Natassia Kelly at http://www.islamonline.net/english/journey/jour3.shtml.

[6]William J. Saal, *Reaching Muslims for Christ* (Chicago: Moody Press, 1993), p. 30.

[7]G. J. O. Moshay, *Who Is this Allah?* (United Kingdom: Dorchester House Publications, 1995), p. 72.

[8]Saal, p. 64.

[9]John Ankerberg and John Weldon, *The Facts on Islam,* (Eugene, Oregon: Harvest House, 1998), pp. 20-21.

AFTERWORD BY U.S. SENATOR
JAMES M. INHOFE

"An Absolute Victory –
America's Stake in Israel's War on Terrorism"

(The following speech is well worth reading! It was made in the United States Senate by U.S. Senator James M. Inhofe (R-Oklahoma) on December 4, 2001. The first two paragraphs have been deleted because they contain material not pertinent to the main body of this book).

Make no mistake about it. This war is first and foremost a spiritual war. It is not a political war. It has never been a political war. It is not about politics. It is a spiritual war. It has its roots in spiritual conflict. It is a war to be fought to destroy the very fabric of our society and the very things for which we stand. Many of the wars in history have been fought because of human desire or greed, to have that of a neighboring country – to have mineral deposits, to have what some other country has. But this war is of a different nature. It is not just simple greed that motivated these people to kill. This war which has been launched against the United States of America is a spiritual attack. It is an attack that was created in the mind and heart of Satan. It is a demonically inspired attack. It is not just the selfish ambitions of an egotistical leader. It is not just someone wanting to hold on to power. *This is nothing more than a satanically inspired attack against America created by demonic powers through the perverted minds of terrorists.*

One may ask: What is it about our Nation that makes them hate us so much? Three things. First, in our country, we have the freedom and the right to choose the kind of worship we want. I am a born-again Christian. I have accepted Jesus Christ as my virtual Lord and Savior. I believe it is through Him that we will reach the Father. I [think] every American has a right to choose whether or not to believe that. Some people have the notion that if you are a Christian who believes in the Bible, you are totally intolerant; you do not allow other people to have a choice. Nothing could be further from the truth. In nations of this world where Christianity is the dominant way of worship, we also find Jewish synagogues, Islamic mosques; we find freedom of worship. But we will not find the same kinds of freedom in the militant Islamic nations of this world. They do not allow Christian churches and Jewish synagogues to operate freely. They do not allow people the freedom of choice. In Sudan, they sell Christians into slavery. So one of the reasons America is hated so much is that we have allowed people through the years to choose what they are going to do. It is choice.

The second reason we are hated is that we have opened the door for people to achieve their God-given place on this Earth. We have not restrained people. We have allowed people freedom of expression, the freedom to pursue dreams, the freedom to pursue goals. This is not true around the world. Freedom did not come cheap.

One of my memories is when I started my education in first grade. It was in a country schoolhouse. Not many people here know what they are. There are eight grades in one room out in the country. I remember three brothers who rode on a workhorse to school every morning. We had a different sense of history at that time. I remember so well reading and learning history as a very young child in that environment.

I remember my teacher said the Pilgrims did not come to this country for adventure; they did not come for excitement; they were not adventurous people. They came to this country to escape tyranny, to pursue freedoms – freedom of religion and economic freedom. Half of them died the first year. They knew it was going to happen. It was worth it to get these freedoms. They had freedom of religion and economic freedom. Each was given a piece of property to do with as they wanted, and [they] could work [their] land and reap the benefits of this property. And [they] prospered mightily, so mightily that in one of his letters back to England, [one of them] said: Now one farmer can grow 10 times as much corn as the previous farmers could. They were prospering so mightily. I normally tell young people when you have a good thing going, quite often someone is going to try to take it away from you. That is exactly what happened. The British came across the sea. They wanted in on this prosperity, and they started imposing laws, rules, and regulations so that the trapper on the frontier could not make a hat of the pelt he caught. He had to sell it to British merchants at British prices to be shipped to Great Britain on English ships to be made into a hat by English laborers to be shipped back and sold to the trapper, who caught it in the first place, at

English prices. Guess what happened. God bless him, the trapper kept right on making his own hats. That was treason in those days. So they sent this great army to this country, the greatest army in the world at that time, to stop these things from occurring. They started marching up toward Lexington and Concord.

I remember so well sitting in that little one-room schoolhouse and having this vision of what it was really like. Farmers and trappers and frontiersmen were up there. They were not well educated, but they were ready to stop this resistance, the greatest army on the face of this Earth. Most of them could not read or write. As the saying goes, they did not know their right foot from their left foot, so they would put a tuft of hay in one boot and a tuft of straw in the other boot and march to the cadence of "hay foot, straw foot." While they were not greatly educated, they knew freedom, and they were going to keep that freedom. As they stood there knowing they were signing their death warrants, those soldiers, listening to the thundering cadence of the largest army in the world going towards Lexington and Concord, waited until they saw the whites of their eyes, and fired the shot heard round the world. At that very moment a tall red haired man named Patrick Henry stood in the House of Burgess and made a speech.

> "There is a just God who presides over the destinies of nations, and who will raise up friends to fight our battles with us. The battle, sir, is not to the strong alone; it is to the vigilant, the active, the brave...Gentlemen may cry, Peace, Peace – but there is no peace...Why stand we here idle? What is it that gentlemen wish? What would they have? Is life so dear, or peace so sweet, as to be purchased at the price of chains and slavery? Forbid it, Almighty God. But as for me, give me liberty or give me death."

He got both.

These freedoms are not found in every nation. America is a great nation because we have magnified the rights of individuals, protected the rights of individuals in our culture. We are careful to allow people to have expression in our society, and we are hated for it.

The third reason we are hated is because we are a nation of laws. We are a people ruled by laws. Lest one thinks that is common, do a careful study of the history of the world. Most of the world's countries do not have a 200-year-old Constitution. They are ruled by dictators. They are ruled by the whims of those leaders or by political parties as they change. The rule of law is what makes civilization possible. The rule of law is what makes an orderly society work. If there is no rule of law, the strongest, toughest bully is the one who runs the country. America is a country of law and order because of the philosophies of the people who founded this Nation. They believed in the rule of law because of what they knew from the Bible. Our Constitution and the constitutions of most of the governments in the world are similar and are indeed based upon the Ten Commandments. *Our fathers knew that the Ten Commandments and the laws of God were a basis for all laws.* They understood the concepts of absolute right and absolute wrong. There were not many who believed in what we today call situational ethics, where things change according to our needs. They believed in absolute right and absolute wrong. America was founded on those principles. That is a reason we are hated so much as a nation. We are hated because of the fact we are a beacon of light, a beacon of freedom all the way around the world. We know contemporarily what this means.

One of the greatest speeches of all times was "A Rendezvous with Destiny" made by Ronald Reagan before he was into politics. He talked about the atrocities committed in Castro's Communist Cuba and about the little boat that escaped and washed up on the southern shores of Florida. When the boat came up, a man who escaped talked about what was happening in Communist Cuba. When he was through talking about the atrocities, a woman said, "I guess we in this country don't know how lucky we are." He said, "No, no. It is how lucky we are because we had a place to escape to."

What he was saying was, we were that beacon of freedom. Many, including the Senator sitting to my right, will remember 15 years ago when the Communists, then the Soviet Union, were trying to get a foothold in Nicaragua and the freedom fighters were fighting for their freedom. I remember going down there, watching them fight against impossible odds. There is no way they could win, by normal concept. There was a hospital tent in Nicaragua. It was half the size of this Senate Chamber. I remember so well, this is where the freedom fighters from Nicaragua would come in and get taken care of medically. There was an operating table in the middle of this giant tent. All they did was amputations. The problem was, of course, the mines. They had the beds of all the patients around the perimeter of

181

this hospital tent. I went around and talked to the individuals. The average age of the fighter in Nicaragua at that time was 19 years old. All the older ones were either maimed or killed. I used to be a pilot in Mexico and I communicate well. I asked each one, "Why is it you are doing this against impossible odds? Why are you doing this? Why are you fighting?" I got to the last bed. The girl in the last bed was named was Maria Gonzalez. I asked her that question. She was 18 years old, weighed 90 pounds, and this was her third trip back to the hospital tent. They amputated her leg that morning. Blood was coming through the bandages. That little girl said, "We are fighting because they have taken everything we have, our farms, our houses, all that we have. Surely you in the United States don't have to ask that question because you had to fight for your freedoms against the same odds that we are doing today. And with God's help, we will win, as you, with God's help, won."

That little girl didn't know whether our Revolution was fought 25 years ago or 150 years ago. But she was brilliant in her knowledge of freedom. We were the beacon of hope. We were the beacon of freedom. Do you know the outcome? We are hated because we are the beacon of freedom for the rest of the world. We are hated because in America we have freedom of choice and freedom of worship, we have freedom of expression, and we are a nation of laws.

Now, why was America attacked on September 11? Why did they single us out? America was attacked because of our system of values. It is a spiritual war. It is not just because we are Israel's best friend. We are Israel's best friend in the world because of the character we have as a nation. We came under attack and we are Israel's best friend.

One of the reasons God has blessed our country is because we have honored His people. Genesis 12:3 says, "I will bless them that bless thee, and curse him that curseth thee." This is God talking about Israel. Madam President, on the table where you sit is a Bible. You can look it up. He said, "I will bless them who bless you. I will curse him who curses you." God is talking about Israel. One of the reasons America has been blessed abundantly over the years is because we as a society have opened our doors to Jewish people. Jewish people have been blessed in the United States of America. When the tiny State of Israel was founded in 1948, we stood in the beginning with Israel. We were the first country to stand up for Israel. Because we took a stand, other nations in the world followed after very quickly. The United States made it possible for there to be an Israel. We stood with Israel again and again and again in its fight to survive.

Make no mistake. It is not just because of our support of Israel. It is what we believe as a nation that caused us to come under attack. Recently in the city of Durban, South Africa, there was a conference called the World Conference on Racism. African Christians are being slaughtered by the thousands today by Islamic [extremists] in Sudan. You didn't hear a lot about that in the reports of this conference; you didn't hear about racism in South Africa. I have a mission in West Africa and have become pretty familiar with some of the atrocities and the ethnic cleansing going on in the world today. I can remember standing at this podium when we were under a different President. He was trying to get us to send troops into Kosovo, and used in his arguments in Kosovo all the ethnic cleansing and the difficulty going on. I said at that time, for every one person who is killed, who is ethnically cleansed in Kosovo, on any given day there are over 100 who are killed and ethnically cleansed in west Africa alone. Do we hear about that? No, we didn't hear about that at the Conference on Racism. What you heard was how the nations of the world came together and decided all the attention should be focused on the tensions in the Middle East. They were appeasing the terrorists.

Israel is under attack in the Middle East because it is the only true democracy that exists in the Middle East. There are more than 20 Arab nations in north Africa and in the Middle East. Virtually every Arab nation is run by either a king or a dictator. Israel is the only true democracy that exists in the Middle East. Madam President, did you know if you are an Arab and have an Israeli citizenship, you can vote in the country of Israel? Did you know the Arabs have parties in the Knesset, the Congress of Israel? *Israel is the only true democracy that exists in the Middle East.* It has a Western form of government based on the laws we see in the Bible. The laws of God that our country is based on are the same laws from which Israel gets its law. It represents the laws of God. That is the reason it is under attack. We ought to be Israel's best friend. If we cannot stand for Israel today, can we ever again be counted on as a beacon of hope, a beacon of freedom for oppressed nations? You may ask what does this have to do with the attack on America? We are under attack because of our character and because we have supported the tiny little nation in the Middle East. That is why we are under attack. If we don't stand for this tiny country today, when do we start standing for tiny little countries in the world that are right?

Yasser Arafat and others do not recognize Israel's right to the land. They don't recognize Israel's right to exist. I will discuss seven things I consider to be indisputable and incontrovertible evidence and grounds to Israel's right to the land. You have heard this before, but it has never been in the RECORD. Most know this. We are going to be hit by skeptics who are going to say we are being attacked all because of our support for Israel, and if we get out of the Middle East all of the problems will go away. That is not so. It is not true. If we withdraw, it will come to our door and will not go away. I have some observations to make about that in just a minute, but first the seven reasons that Israel has the right to the land.

Israel has a right to the land because of all the archeological evidence. This is reason No. 1. It all supports it. Every time there is a dig in Israel, it does nothing but support the fact that Israelis have had a presence there for 3,000 years. They have been there for a long time. The coins, the cities, the pottery, the culture – there are other people, groups that are there, but there is no mistaking the fact that Israelis have been present in that land for 3,000 years. It predates any claims that other peoples in the regions may have. The ancient Philistines are extinct. Many other ancient peoples are extinct. They do not have the unbroken line to this date that the Israelis have. Even the Egyptians of today are not the racial Egyptians of 3,000 years ago. They are primarily an Arab people. The land is called Egypt, but they are not the same racial and ethnic stock as the Old Egyptians of the ancient world. The Israelis are in fact descended from the original Israelites. The first proof, then, is archeology.

The second proof of Israel's right to the land is the historic right. History supports it totally and completely. We know there has been an Israel up until the time of the Roman Empire. The Romans conquered the land. Israel had no homeland, although Jews were allowed to live there. They were driven from the land in two dispersions: One was in 70 A.D. and the other was in 135 A.D. But there was always a Jewish presence in the land. The Turks, who took over about 700 years ago and ruled the land up until about World War I, had control. Then the land was conquered by the British. The Turks entered World War I on the side of Germany. The British knew they had to do something to punish Turkey and also to break up that empire that was going to be a part of the whole effort of Germany in

World War I, so the British sent troops against the Turks in the Holy Land.

The general who was leading the British armies was a man named Allenby. Allenby was a Bible-believing Christian. He carried a Bible with him everywhere he went and he knew the significance of Jerusalem. The night before the attack against Jerusalem to drive out the Turks, Allenby prayed that God would allow him to capture the city without doing damage to the holy places. That day, Allenby sent World War I biplanes over the city of Jerusalem to do a reconnaissance mission. You have to understand that the Turks had at that time never seen an airplane. So there they were, flying around. They looked in the sky and saw these fascinating inventions and did not know what they were and they were terrified by them. Then they were told that they were being opposed by a man named Allenby the next day, which in their language means "man sent from God" or "prophet from God." They dared not fight against a prophet from God, so the next morning when Allenby went to take Jerusalem, he went in and captured it without firing a single shot.

The British Government was grateful to Jewish people around the world and particularly to one Jewish chemist who helped them with the manufacture of niter. Niter is an ingredient which goes into nitroglycerin, necessary to the war effort. They were getting dangerously low of niter in England at that time, so the chemist, who was called Weizmann, discovered a way to make it from materials that existed in England. It was coming from the new world over there, the niter was. But the German U-boats were shooting them down so it was all at the bottom of the Atlantic Ocean. When Weizmann discovered a way to make it from materials that existed in England, it saved the British war effort. Out of gratitude to this Jew and out of gratitude to Jewish bankers and financiers and others who lent financial support, England said we are going to set aside a homeland in the Middle East for the Jewish people. And that is history.

The homeland that Britain said it would set aside consisted of all of what is now Israel and all of what was then the nation of Jordan, the whole thing. That was what Britain promised to give the Jews in 1917. In the beginning, there was some Arab support for this. There was not a huge Arab population in the land at that time and there is a reason for that. The land was not able to sustain a large population of people. It just didn't have the development it needed to handle all those people, and the land wasn't really wanted by anybody.

I want you to listen to Mark Twain. Have you ever read "Huckleberry Finn" or "Tom Sawyer"? Mark Twain (Samuel Clemens) took a tour of Palestine in 1867. This is how he described it. We are talking about Israel. He said:

> "A desolate country whose soil is rich enough but is given over wholly to weeds. A silent, mournful expanse. We never saw a human being on the whole route. There was hardly a tree or a shrub anywhere. Even the olive and the cactus, those fast friends of a worthless soil, had almost deserted the country."

Where was this great Palestinian nation? It didn't exist. It wasn't there. The Palestinians weren't there. Palestine was a region named by the Romans, but at the time it was under the control of Turkey and there was no large mass of people there because the land would not support them.

This is the report of the Palestinian Royal Commission, created by the British. It quotes an account of the conditions on the coastal plain, along the Mediterranean Sea in 1913. This is the Palestinian Royal Commission. They said:

> "The road leading from Gaza to the north was only a summer track, suitable for transport by camels or carts. No orange groves, orchards or vineyards were to be seen until one reached the Yavnev village. Houses were mud. Schools did not exist. The western part toward the sea was almost a desert. The villages in this area were few and thinly populated. Many villages were deserted by their inhabitants."

The French author Voltaire described Palestine as "A hopeless, dreary place."

In short, under the Turks the land suffered from neglect and low population, and that is an historical fact. The nation became populated with both Jews and Arabs because the land came to prosper when Jews came back and began to reclaim it. Historically, they began to reclaim it. If there had never been any archeological evidence at all to support the rights of the Israelis to the territory, it is also important to recognize that other nations in the area have no longstanding claim to the country either.

Madam President, did you know that Saudi Arabia was not created until 1913? Lebanon until 1920? Iraq didn't exist as a nation until 1932; Syria until 1941; the borders of Jordan were established in 1946, and Kuwait in 1961. Any of these nations who would say that Israel is only a recent arrival would have to deny their own rights as recent arrivals as well. They did not exist as countries. They were all under the control of the Turks. So, historically, Israel gained its independence in 1948.

The third reason I believe the land belongs to Israel is because of the practical value of the Israelis being there. Israel today is a modern marvel of agriculture. Israel is able to bring more food out of a desert environment than any other country in the world. The Arab nations ought to make Israel their friend and import technology from Israel that would allow all the Middle East, not just Israel, to become an exporter of food. Israel has unarguable success in its agriculture.

The fourth reason I believe Israel has the right to the land is on the grounds of humanitarian concern. You see, there were 6 million Jews slaughtered in Europe in World War II. The persecution against the Jews has been very strong in Russia since the advent of communism. It was against them even before then under the Czars. These people have a right to their homeland. If we are not going to allow them a homeland in the Middle East, then where? What other nation on Earth is going to cede territory? To give up land? They are not asking for a great deal. You know the whole nation of Israel would fit into my State of Oklahoma seven times. So on humanitarian grounds alone, Israel ought to have the land.

The fifth reason Israel ought to have the land is because she is a strategic ally to the United States. Whether we realize it or not, Israel is a detriment, an impediment to certain groups hostile to democracies and hostile to those things that we believe in, hostile to the very things that make us the greatest nation in the history of the world. They have kept them from taking complete control of the Middle East. If it were not for Israel, they would overrun the region. They are our strategic ally. Madam President, it is good to know that we have a friend in the Middle East that we can count on. They vote with us in the United Nations more than England. They vote with us more than Canada, more than France, more than Germany, more than any other country in the world.

The sixth reason is that Israel is a roadblock to terrorism. The war we are now facing is not against a sovereign nation. It is a group of terrorists who are very fluid, moving from one country to another. They are almost invisible. That is who we are fighting against. We need every ally we can get. If we do not stop terrorism in the Middle East, it will be on our shores. We have said this and said this and said this. One of the reasons I believe the spiritual door was opened for an attack against the United States of America is because the policy of our Government has been to ask Israelis and demand with pressure that they not retaliate in a significant way against the terrorist strikes that have been launched against them, the most recent one just 2 days ago.

Since its independence in 1948, Israel has fought four wars: the war in 1948-1949; the war in 1956, the Sinai campaign; the Six-Day War in 1967; and in 1973 the Yom Kippur War, the holiest day of the year, with Egypt and Syria. You have to understand that in all four cases, Israel was attacked. Some people may argue that wasn't true because they went in first in the war of 1956. But they knew at that time that Egypt was building a huge military to become the aggressor. Israel, in fact, was not the aggressor and has not been the aggressor in any of the four wars. Also, they won all four wars against impossible odds. They are great warriors. They consider a level playing field being outnumbered two to one.

There were 39 Scud missiles that landed on Israeli soil during the Gulf War. Our President asked Israel not to respond. In order to have the Arab nations on board, we asked Israel not even to participate in the war. They showed tremendous restraint and did not. And now we've asked them to stand back and not do anything over these last several attacks. We have criticized them. We have criticized them in our media. Local people in television and radio offer criticisms of Israel not knowing the true issues. We need to be informed.

I was so thrilled when I heard a reporter pose a question to our Secretary of State, Colin Powell. He said, "Mr. Powell, the United States has advocated a policy of restraint in the Middle East. We have discouraged Israel from retaliation again and again, and again because we've said it leads to continued escalation – that it escalates the violence." He said, "Are we going to follow that preaching ourselves?" Mr. Powell indicated that we would strike back. In other words, we can tell Israel not to do it, but when it hits us we are going to do something. That is one of the reasons I believe the door was opened. Because we have held back our tiny little friend. We have not allowed them to go to the heart of the problem. The heart of the problem – that is where we are going now. But all that changed yesterday when the Israelis went into the Gaza with gunships and into the West Bank with F-16s. With the exception of last May, the Israelis had not used F-16s since the 1967 7-Day War. And I am so proud of them because we have to stop terrorism. It is not going to go away. If Israel were driven into the sea tomorrow, if every Jew in the Middle East were killed, terrorism would not end. You know that in your heart. Terrorism would continue. It is not just a matter of Israel in the Middle East. It is the heart of the very people who are perpetrating this stuff. Should they be successful in overrunning Israel – they won't be – but should they be, it would not be enough. They will never be satisfied.

Seventhly, I believe very strongly that we ought to support Israel; that it has a right to the land. This is the most important reason: Because God said so. As I said a minute ago, look it up in the book of Genesis. In Genesis 13:14-17, the Bible says:

> "And the Lord said unto Abram, Lift up now thine eyes, and look from the place where thou art northward, and southward, and eastward, and westward: For all the land which thou seest, to thee will I give it, and to thy seed forever... Arise, walk through the land in the length of it and in the breadth of it; for I will give it unto thee."

That is God talking.

The Bible says that Abram removed his tent, and came and dwelt in the plain of Mamre, which is in Hebron, and built there an altar before the Lord. Hebron is in the West Bank. It is at this place where God appeared to Abram and said, "I am giving you this land," – the West Bank. This is not a political battle at all. It is a contest over whether or not the word of God is true. The seven reasons here, I am convinced, clearly establish that Israel has a right to the land.

Eight years ago on the lawn of the White House, Yitzhak Rabin shook hands with PLO Chairman, Yasser Arafat. It was an historic occasion. It was also a tragic occasion. At that time, the official policy of the Government of Israel began to be, "Let us appease the terrorists. Let us begin to trade the land for peace." This process has continued unabated up until last year. Here in our own Nation, at Camp David, in the summer of 2000, then Prime Minister of Israel, Ehud Barak, offered the most generous concessions to Yasser Arafat that had ever been laid on the table. He offered him more than 90 percent of all the West Bank territory; sovereign control of it. There were some parts he did not want to offer, but in exchange for that he said he would give up land in Israel proper that the PLO was not asking for. And he also did the unthinkable. He even spoke of dividing Jerusalem and allowing the Palestinians to have their capital there in the East. Yasser Arafat stormed out of the meeting. Why did he storm out of the meeting? Everything he has said he has wanted all of these years was put into his hand. Why did he storm out of the meeting?

A couple of months later, there began to be riots, terrorism. The riots began when, now Prime Minister, Ariel Sharon, went to the Temple Mount. And this was used as the thing that lit the fire and that caused the explosion. Did you know that Sharon did not go unannounced and that he contacted the Islamic authorities before he went and secured their permission and had permission to be there? It was no surprise. The response was very carefully calculated. They knew the world would not pay attention to the details. They would portray this in the Arab world as an attack upon the holy mosque. They would portray it as an attack upon that mosque and use it as an excuse to riot. Over the last eight years, during this time of the peace process, where the Israeli public has pressured its leaders to give up land for peace because they're tired of fighting, there has been increased terror. In fact, it has been greater in the last eight years than any other time in Israel's history. Showing restraint and giving in has not produced any kind of peace. It is so much so, that today the leftist peace movement in Israel does not exist because the people feel they were deceived.

They did offer a hand of peace, and it was not taken. That is why the politics of Israel have changed drastically over the past 12 months. The Israelis have come to see that, "No matter what we do, these people do not want to deal with us...They want to destroy us." That is why even yet today the stationery of the PLO still has upon it the map of the entire state of Israel, not just the tiny little part they call the West Bank that they want. They want it all.

190

The unwavering loyalty we have received from our only consistent friend in the Middle East has got to be respected and appreciated by us. No longer should foreign policy in the Middle East be one of appeasement. As Hiram Mann said, "No man survives when freedom fails. The best men rot in filthy jails and those who cried 'appease, appease' are hanged by those they tried to please."

Islamic...terrorism has now come to America. We have to use all of our friends, all of our assets, and all of our resources to defeat the satanic evil. When Patrick Henry said, "We will not fight our battles alone. There is a just God who reigns over the destiny of nations who will raise up friends who will fight our battles with us," he was talking about all our friends, including Israel. And that is what is happening, as of yesterday and I thank God for that. Israel is now in the battle by our side. That is what is happening. As of yesterday, Israel is now in the battle by our side, and I thank God for that. It is time for our policy of appeasement in the Middle East and appeasement to the terrorists to be over. With our partners, our victory must and will be absolute victory.

BIBLIOGRAPHY OF
BOOKS AND PERIODICALS

Books

Ankerberg, John and Weldon, John. *The Facts on Islam.* Eugene, Oregon: Harvest House, 1998.

Ankerberg, John and Weldon, John. *Fast Facts on Islam.* Eugene, Oregon: Harvest House, 2001.

Caner, Ergun and Caner, Emir. *Unveiling Islam: An Insider's Look at Muslim Life and Beliefs.* Grand Rapids, Michigan: Kregel Publications, 2002.

Cairns, Earle E. *Christianity Through the Centuries.* Grand Rapids, Michigan: Zondervan, 1981.

Chalabian, Antranig. *Armenia After the Coming of Islam.* Southfield, Michigan: Antranig Chalabian, 1999.

Churchill, Winston S. "Holiday Time," in *Winston S. Churchill, Volume V, 1922-1939*, by Martin Gilbert. London: Heinemann, 1976, p. 1099.

DeHaan, M. R. *Coming Events in Prophecy.* Grand Rapids, Michigan: Zondervan Publishing House, 1962.

DeHaan, M. R. *Signs of the Times.* Grand Rapids, Michigan: Zondervan Publishing House, 1951.

El Schafi, Abd. *Behind the Veil: Unmasking Islam.* Abd El Schafi, 2000.

Geisler, Norman. *Baker Encyclopedia of Christian Apologetics.* Grand Rapids, Michigan: Baker Book House, 2000.

Gilbert, Martin. *Winston S. Churchill, Volume V, 1922-1939.* London: Heinemann, 1976. Includes "Holiday Time" speech by Churchill on page 1099.

Graham, Billy. *World Aflame.* Garden City, New York: Doubleday & Company, 1965.

Hymers, R. L., Jr. and Cagan, Christopher. *Today's Apostasy.* Oklahoma City, Oklahoma: Hearthstone Publishing, second edition, 2001.

Jamieson, Robert; Fausset, Andrew; and Brown, David. *Jamieson, Fausset, and Brown* commentary. Grand Rapids, Michigan: William B. Eerdmans Publishing Co., reprinted 1976.

Keil, C. F. and Delitzsch, F. *Commentary on the Old Testament.* 10 volumes. Grand Rapids, Michigan: William B. Eerdmans Publishing Co., 1973.

Koch, Kurt. *Occult ABC.* Germany: Literature Missions, 1983.

MacArthur, John F., Jr., ed. *MacArthur Study Bible.* Nashville: Thomas Nelson.

Marshall, Paul. *Their Blood Cries Out.* Waco, Texas: Word Publishing, 1997.

Mayor, Joseph P. *The Epistle of St. Jude and the 2nd Epistle of St. Peter.* Grand Rapids, Michigan: Baker Book House, 1965.

Moshay, G. J. O. *Who Is This Allah?* United Kingdom: Dorchester House Publications, 1995.

Nevius, John. *Demon Possession and Allied Themes.* Old Tappan, New Jersey: Fleming H. Revell, 1894.

Pardington, George P. *Outline Studies in Christian Doctrine.* Christian Publications, 1926.

Reinecker, Fritz. *A Linguistic Key to the Greek New Testament.* Grand Rapids, Michigan: Zondervan Publishing House, 1980.

Rice, John R. *Our God-Breathed Book: The Bible.* Murfreesboro, Tennessee: Sword of the Lord, 1969.

Rice, John R. "America Gets Back Her Scrap Iron," sermon in *When Skeletons Come Out of Their Closets.* Murfreesboro, Tennessee, Sword of the Lord, 1943.

Ryrie, Charles C., ed. *Ryrie Study Bible.* Northfield Publications.

Saal, William J. *Reaching Muslims for Christ.* Chicago: Moody Press, 1993.

Schaeffer, Francis A. *How Should We Then Live?* Old Tappan, New Jersey: Fleming H. Revell, 1976.

Schaff, Philip. *A History of the Christian Church.* 6 volumes. Grand Rapids: William B. Eerdmans Publishing Co., 1976.

Smith, Huston. *The World's Great Religions.* San Francisco: Harper, 1992.

Strong, Augustus H. *Systematic Theology.* Valley Forge, Pennsylvania: Judson Press, 1985.

Thiessen, Henry C. *Lectures in Systematic Theology.* Grand Rapids, Michigan: William B. Eerdmans Publishing Co., 1963.

Unger, Merrill F. *Biblical Demonology.* Chicago: Scripture Press, 1952.

Unger, Merrill F. *Unger's Commentary on the Old Testament.* Chicago: Moody Press, 1981.

Waite, D. A. *Halloween – The Devil's Birthday.* Oklahoma City, Oklahoma: Southwest Radio Church, n.d.
Walvoord, John F. *The Bible Knowledge Commentary.* 2 volumes. Victor Books, 1985.

Periodicals

Ashcroft, John. Statement in *Christianity Today,* April 1, 2002.
Boston Herald, September 13, 2001, column by Don Feder.
California Southern Baptist, July 2002, statement by Jerry Vines, page 8.
Christian History, May 2002, issue 74, article "Divided by Christ" by Samuel Hugh Moffett, p. 40.
Christianity Today, April 1, 2002, statement by John Ashcroft.
Falwell, Jerry. *National Liberty Journal,* July 2002, pp. 2-3.
Feder, Don. Column in the *Boston Herald*, September 13, 2001.
Globe, October 6, 2001, pp. 1-2.
Los Angeles Daily News, October 23, 2001, p. 7.
Los Angeles Times, November 11, 2001, p. A-1.
Moffett, Samuel Hugh. "Divided by Christ," *Christian History,* May 2002, issue 74, p. 40.
National Liberty Journal, July 2002, statement by Jerry Falwell, pages 2 and 3.
Newsweek, December 13, 2001, pp. 2, 5.
Time, "What's Next?" November 5, 2001, pp. 44-45.
Time, "The Taliban Next Door." December 17, 2001, pp. 36-38.
Time, June 24, 2002, pp. 28-32.
U.S. News and World Report, June 10, 2002, p. 17.
Vines, Jerry. *California Southern Baptist,* July 2002, p. 8.
Yamauchi, Edwin M. "Historical Notes on the Incomparable Christ," *Christianity Today,* October 22, 1971, pp. 7-11.